on track ...
Van Halen

every album, every song

Morgan Brown

sonicbondpublishing.com

Sonicbond Publishing Limited
www.sonicbondpublishing.co.uk
Email: info@sonicbondpublishing.co.uk

First Published in the United Kingdom 2023
First Published in the United States 2023

British Library Cataloguing in Publication Data:
A Catalogue record for this book is available from the British Library

Copyright Morgan Brown 2023

ISBN 978-1-78952-256-3

Typeset in ITC Garamond & ITC Avant Garde
Printed and bound in England

Graphic design and typesetting: Full Moon Media

on track ...
Van Halen

every album, every song

Morgan Brown

sonicbondpublishing.com

Follow us on social media:
Twitter: https://twitter.com/SonicbondP
Instagram: https://www.instagram.com/sonicbondpublishing_/
Facebook: https://www.facebook.com/SonicbondPublishing/

Linktree QR code:

Acknowlegements

This book is dedicated to the memory of Rob and
Wendy Brown, my wonderful parents, who nurtured
my passion for music with love and patience.

I would like to thank Stephen Lambe of Sonicbond
Publishing for giving me this opportunity to translate
a lifetime's fandom into written form. I am also
grateful to Brad Tolinksi and Chris Gill, Greg Renoff
and John Scanlan for their superb books, which were
invaluable sources of background information.

Lastly, I would like to thank Van Halen for
their inspirational music, which has changed
so many lives, mine included.

on track ...

Van Halen

Contents

Strong magic comin' on!

Arguably the greatest rock band the US has ever produced, over the course of 12 studio albums, two live records and a couple of compilations, Van Halen irrevocably changed the course of guitar-based popular music. Their vibrant, energised take on heavy rock revitalised a genre that was becoming stodgy and staid, in danger of being smothered by its own cliches. By melding the essential elements of hard rock – huge riffs, flashy solos, pummelling rhythms and wailing vocals – with the raw, snotty energy of punk and a razor-sharp pop sensibility, Van Halen created an exciting and wildly successful hybrid, often emulated, but never equalled. Moreover, the individual band members were each remarkable in their own right: Eddie Van Halen, the visionary guitarist and composer who almost singlehandedly brought about a new epoch of musicianship and guitar design; Alex Van Halen, whose unique blend of jazzy finesse and pugnacious power were the perfect match for his brother's unbridled creativity; David Lee Roth, the pop-cultural magpie and supreme showman, counterbalancing the brothers' introverted musicianship with irrepressible star power; and Michael Anthony, the underrated everyman, whose lively, rock-solid bass work and note-perfect harmonies provided the ideal foundation for the band's flights of fancy.

The Van Halen family – jazz musician Jan, his Dutch-Indonesian wife Eugenia and their two sons, Edward and Alex – arrived in the USA from the Netherlands in 1962, settling in a working-class area of Pasadena. While their father struggled to find gigs and made ends meet with janitorial work, the boys, struggling to assimilate in their new, English-speaking surroundings, formed an especially tight bond with one another. Both parents were keen for their offspring to pursue music, sending their sons for violin and piano lessons. However, classical music couldn't match the lure of surf music and the new British beat boom sound, and soon the boys took up paper rounds to save for instruments more suitable for rock n' roll. Alex started on guitar and Edward on drums, but when Eddie showed more natural six-string proficiency than Alex, they made the fateful swap. After a couple of short-lived earlier bands, the brothers made their first major foray into the rock world with Genesis, soon to be renamed Mammoth when they became aware of the UK band of the same name. The band's line-up settled with the brothers being joined by bassist Mark Stone and, later, keyboardist Jim Pewsey. They quickly made a name for themselves on the Pasadena backyard party circuit, with their astonishingly accurate renditions of the era's heavy rock favourites – Black Sabbath, Deep Purple, Ten Years After etc. Their instrumental abilities were immediately impressive, but Eddie was a reluctant vocalist, and the band's image and stage presence were practically non-existent.

Enter David Lee Roth, a supremely self-confident motormouth, whose family had moved to Southern California in 1963. Roth had a burning conviction that he was destined to be a rock star and recognised the Van

Halen brothers as his ticket to that destination. Unfortunately, initially, his ambition far outstripped his abilities, and he failed his audition for the brothers. Undeterred, Dave honed his act in his own group, Red Ball Jet, whose funk/R&B influences were a marked contrast to Mammoth's po-faced monolithic riffs and extended solos. Red Ball Jet didn't last long, but during their existence, Roth acquired a PA system which he rented to Mammoth, gradually using this to leverage his way into the band. While the brothers were still not impressed with Roth's voice, Eddie was keen to escape lead vocal responsibilities and save money on PA hire to boot, so they grudgingly gave him a chance. Dave's vocal abilities may not have been the strongest – even years later, in his riotous autobiography, *Crazy from the Heat*, he self-deprecatingly likens his voice to 'four flat tires on a muddy road'. However, he more than made up for any deficiencies with his peerless charisma, drive, showmanship and commercial nous. The band's live shows instantly became infinitely more entertaining, with Roth's stage persona, initially modelled after Black Oak Arkansas's Jim 'Dandy' Mangrum, soon taking on a life of its own. With Roth taking the promotional reins, the band's following grew, moving beyond the increasingly huge parties they had been playing to clubs and bars, and, eventually, to Hollywood's Sunset strip. The band metamorphosed, with Pewsey quitting in disgust at Roth's onstage antics, and Mark Stone being replaced by ex-Sniper bassist/vocalist Michael Anthony Sobelewski – an excellent player and superb harmony singer with a grounded, unassuming attitude. It was Roth who suggested the name change to Van Halen, after it again emerged that another band was already using Mammoth. Santana had set a precedent for naming a group after its guitarist, and this striking, unique moniker set them apart from the hordes of other Southern California backyard hopefuls. Although they had a lot of hard work ahead of them, and some crushing disappointments – notably an abortive spell under the managerial wing of Kiss bassist Gene Simmons – they were now on the path that would lead them to world-conquering status.

Over years of spectacular highs and stomach-churning lows, conflicts and reconciliations, glorious triumphs and heart-breaking failures, they produced a body of work that includes some of the finest records in the history of rock music – songs that have soundtracked millions of great nights out and spawned millions of aspiring guitar heroes. In this book, I hope to go some way towards explaining, song by song, how a backyard covers band from Pasadena tore up the rock rule book and changed the face of popular music forever.

Van Halen (1978)

Personnel:
David Lee Roth: lead vocals, acoustic guitar on 'Ice Cream Man'
Edward Van Halen: guitar, backing vocals
Michael Anthony: bass, backing vocals
Alex Van Halen: drums
Recorded at Sunset Sound Recorders, Hollywood
Produced by Ted Templeman
Engineered by Donn Landee
Record label: Warner Brothers
Release date: 10 February 1978
Highest chart position: US: 19, UK: 34
Running time: 35:34
Current edition: 2019 reissue

1977 was a difficult year to be an up-and-coming LA hard rock band. The initial wave of heavy acts who revolutionised rock in the late 1960s had largely either split or become bloated shadows of their former selves. The clubs of Hollywood's Sunset Strip, once a counter-cultural focal point, now hired top-40 cover bands to fill emptying dancefloors, while the rock stars who had once populated them retreated to their Laurel Canyon mansions. The first rumblings of the Los Angeles punk scene had begun, but overall, it seemed as though the party of the late sixties and early seventies had moved on, not to return.

In this setting, Warner Brothers' Vice-President Ted Templeman and Chairman Mo Austin's experience of a Van Halen live show (at the Starwood club in May, 1977) must have been especially startling. Here was a young band whose power and musicianship easily outstripped any of their hard-rock contemporaries, possessing a flamboyance and charisma not seen since the heyday of glam, and channelling a reckless energy that resonated with the burgeoning punk movement. The years of Pasadena backyard parties and long nights at Gazzarri's on the Strip had honed them into a slick, assured act with a jaw-dropping guitarist, a magnetic frontman, and a sound compressing key elements of rock's past, present and future into compact, danceable gems – hits, in other words.

Contracts were signed, and in October, recording of the band's self-titled debut album commenced, with Templeman producing, and his long-time collaborator, Donn Landee engineering. Templeman, a former pop star himself with Harper's Bazaar, had an impressive production CV, including key albums by Van Morrison, Little Feat, and Montrose. Guitarist Ronnie Montrose's eponymous heavy rockers were an early influence on Van Halen, and featured vocals from one Sam Hagar, who would later play a huge role in the Van Halen story. In creating the signature sound of *Van Halen*, Templeman took the same approach he had used on Montrose's self-titled debut (1973), focusing on capturing the band's live sound with minimal overdubbing or studio trickery. Throughout the album, the bass and drums are in the centre of the stereo field, with guitar panned to the left channel. To fill out the sound, Templeman treated the guitar tracks with Sunset Sound's distinctive plate reverb, panning the reverb signal hard right, creating a much broader overall effect. This was topped with Roth's freewheeling lead vocal, Eddie and Michael's distinctive harmonies, the occasional second guitar track and little more – a surprisingly simple recipe for such a huge-sounding record.

Prior to starting the album, Templeman and Landee had cut a mammoth 28-song demo with the band, recording their entire repertoire at the time in a single two-hour session. This allowed Templeman to get a sense of how the band worked in the studio, and gauge which songs would be suitable for their debut. Many that didn't initially make the cut would be revised or cannibalised over the years, with fragments or even whole songs from the demo still finding their way onto Van Halen LPs decades later. On a creative high, they concocted a further five new songs in the interim between demo and LP. Ultimately, for the first outing, Templeman and the band settled on seven originals (four of which were from the freshly-composed batch), a supercharged version of the Kinks' 'You Really Got Me', a rollicking take on John Brim's Chicago blues shuffle, 'Ice Cream Man', and 'Eruption' – an instrumental, not initially slated for inclusion on the album, that became one of the band's most emblematic pieces. At just over 35 minutes, and with no songs hitting the four-minute mark, it was a strikingly concise, impactful statement, at a time when meandering indulgence tarnished the work of many of rock's old guard.

The album was finished in three weeks, and cost around $54,000 to produce – a not inconsiderable sum, but paltry compared to the era's mega-budget major-label releases (Fleetwood Mac's *Tusk* (1979), for instance, cost over $1 million). The front cover featured photographs of the band members in action on a darkened stage, leaving blurry trails of colour in their wake. Eddie brandishes his distinctive black and white striped 'Frankenstein' guitar, an inspired, home-made hybrid, using a Fender style body fitted with a Gibson Humbucker pickup and, later, a Floyd Rose locking vibrato, instantly spawning a herd of copycats; Meanwhile, Roth, bare-chested, in tight leather pants, holds his mic at crotch height in a gesture of unambiguous machismo. In the centre, shone the band's iconic 'winged VH' logo, created by David Bhang. The album was preceded by the single 'You Really Got Me', which reached a respectable number 36 on the *Billboard* Hot 100. The album followed in February, rising to number 19 in the US chart, and 34 in the UK. Contemporary reviews were generally cautiously positive, although some critics were reluctant to admit to enjoying a record so openly joyous and lacking in intellectual pretension. Nevertheless, the record has only grown in stature over the years and is now widely considered to be a genre-redefining masterpiece and one of the greatest hard rock albums of all time.

'Runnin' with the Devil' (Van Halen, Van Halen, Roth, Anthony)

Van Halen's recording career begins with an eerie, air raid siren-like howl, increasing in volume as it descends in pitch. This synthesizer-like sound was, in fact, produced by car horns, removed from the band members' own vehicles, electronically processed and pitch-shifted on tape. It's a striking start to the record, evoking both the constant, angry buzz of traffic on the nearby LA freeway, and the siren that wails over the opening riff of Black Sabbath's 'War Pigs' (1970), a notable early influence. The klaxon is cut off by thudding, metronomic bass notes, played on the open low E (actually E flat, because the band are tuned down by a semitone, as they remained throughout the Roth era). Anthony's tone is a rich growl, filling up the sonic space a rhythm guitar track might occupy in other bands. Eddie runs his pick across the strings behind the nut for a tinkling wind-chime effect, and then hits the main riff.

'Runnin' with the Devil' is powerful but controlled. Its stately mid-tempo groove is noticeably slower than earlier demo versions, suggesting that Templeman reined in the band's irrepressible energy a tad. The crunching bass pedal note continues, over which the guitar plays a two-bar series of rising chords, eventually landing on E in unison with the bass, before the pattern is punctuated with a slashing fretboard slide and a cymbal crash. It's dramatic and impactful but not overblown, and only Dave's trademark shriek hints at the reckless abandon to come. The volume drops for the verse, as Roth takes centre stage. Some critics deride Roth's lyrics as crude or lacking depth. Roth himself dismissed the idea that lyrics should strive to be meaningful or 'artistic' in his autobiography:

> There are certain things that shouldn't have too much meaning, like Saturday night. Don't overload it, you know. If your message is that important, use Western Union.

Nevertheless, for all his insouciance, Roth's lyrics are carefully crafted, economical exercises in myth-building and storytelling, and 'Runnin' with the Devil' is no exception. Over two short verses, he vividly paints the self-image that would endure throughout his career – the archetypal hard-living, hard-partying lone wolf: 'I live my life like there's no tomorrow… I'm living at a pace that kills'. The second verse adds some autobiography to the self-mythology, stating that 'I got no love, no love you'd call real / Ain't got nobody waitin' at home'. Roth has spoken in interviews and in his book about the single-minded isolation he felt from early childhood, and while his bandmates would all marry and attempt to settle down over the years, Roth remained single, suggesting that his lyrics reveal more truth and vulnerability than he might admit.

The chorus consists of the title repeated in two-part harmony, with Anthony's distinctive high vocal providing a poppy brightness far removed from the gruff machismo of many heavy rock bands. Over this, Roth works himself into a frenzy of whoops and exhortations owing more to soul and gospel vocal traditions than white-boy rock. The phrase 'Runnin' with the Devil' tips its hat to rock's long-standing flirtation with the dark side, dating back to early classics like Gene Vincent's 'Race with the Devil' (1956), and originating in the central myth of the blues – Robert Johnson's pact with the devil at the crossroads. However, if Johnson was haunted by his satanic dalliance, as 'Hellhound on my Trail' (1937) suggests, Van Halen embrace theirs – running *with* not *from* their demons. Given the lyrical content, we might expect the melody to be correspondingly bluesy, but it's actually based on the Mixolydian mode – a major scale with a flattened 7th. This creates a sound that's brighter and more melodic than any post-Cream/Zeppelin blues rock while fiercer and gutsier than the radio-friendly AOR of Journey or REO Speedwagon.

Following the second and third choruses, Eddie overdubs a guitar solo, panned to the right. When recording single-guitar bands, it has long been common practice to double the rhythm guitar, panning the tracks left and right for a fuller sound, and overdubbing lead breaks on a separate track, avoiding a fall-off in dynamics during the move from chords to single notes. The 1976 Gene Simmons-produced demo of the song took this approach, creating a denser but less dynamic sound. On the LP, a single guitar track does most of the work, moving seamlessly from chords to lead trills and flurries of harmonics. Only on extended lead breaks does the main track keep playing a power-chord and pick-slide rhythm, while the overdubbed lead plays a catchy, simple melodic line, based on the A and G major scales and arpeggios. Everything is played with Eddie's trademark 'brown sound' – the distinctive, warm overdrive he created by lowering the voltage of his Marshall amp, using a Variac – and with his customary flair. However, by Van Halen standards, it's relatively restrained, with the real fireworks held in reserve for the next track.

By the second instrumental, the tempo increases noticeably as a sense of excitement grows, and the extended final chorus is enlivened by some rhythmic changes, with Alex punctuating each bass note with a sharp cymbal grab. A stomping double-time section with Roth unleashing a series of wild falsetto whoops reaches a feral climax, before more cymbal grabs and a flurry of tom-toms provide a tight finish. Released as the album's second single in April 1978, 'Runnin' with the Devil' didn't exactly set the charts alight, reaching number 54 in the UK and 82 in the US. Nevertheless, it fared better in the brothers' native Netherlands, reaching number eight in the Dutch top 40, and is widely regarded as one of the band's finest moments.

'Eruption' (Van Halen, Van Halen, Roth, Anthony)

Here's where the fireworks come in! It's bizarre to think that 'Eruption', the piece that first brought Eddie's astonishing abilities to the attention of the wider world, was not initially intended for inclusion on the album. Templeman overheard him practising his solo spot for an upcoming live set in-between takes, and recognised the impact it could have on the album. Eddie was surprised by the producer's interest, but the band dutifully laid down a few versions, and the chosen take went on to change rock guitar forever.

The opening section, featuring crashing, declamatory chords played by the full band, interspersed with bursts of lead, is cheekily borrowed from 'Let Me Swim' (1970) by Cactus, an act frequently covered by Mammoth. Eddie's tone is lent an ethereal swirling quality by his MXR Phase 90 pedal. His playing is staggeringly speedy, but also deeply expressive, peppered with squealing pinch harmonics (a technique popularised on electric guitar by ZZ Top's Billy Gibbons), and death-defying vibrato bar divebombs, performed with an abandon not heard since the similarly-revolutionary early recordings of Jimi Hendrix. You can hear blues roots, but expressed in a bold, futuristic manner, far removed from the purism of Eddie's stated primary influence, Eric Clapton.

Prior to his discovery of the blues rock of Cream and their ilk, Eddie was initially inspired to play guitar by the quintessential Californian sound of surf music, and there may be a touch of surf legend Dick Dale's influence in the machine gun tremolo picking that follows. The hummingbird-like buzz and warbling left-hand trills ramp up tension towards the titular 'Eruption'. This arrives as a rising sequence of arpeggios, sounding more like an excerpt from a Bach organ work than anything previously heard in hard rock. It's executed at an astonishing and at the time, inexplicable pace, thanks to Eddie's two-handed tapping technique – using both hands on the fretboard, so that all the notes of an arpeggio can be played on a single string with remarkable speed and fluidity. Eddie was not the first to experiment with two-handed fretting. Early examples of similar techniques can be heard on Frank Zappa's 'Inca Roads' (1975) and Steve Hackett's solo on 'The Musical Box' (1971) by Genesis. In his thorough and evocative study of the band's early years, *Van Halen Rising,* Greg Renoff suggests that Eddie learned the two-handed technique from his friend, Terry Kilgore, who took lessons from ex-Canned Heat virtuoso Harvey Mandel, a tapping pioneer since at least 1973. However, nobody had ever come close to developing the technique so fully, integrating it so completely into their style, or using it with such musicality as Eddie. After the organ-like tapping section resolves harmonically, the track concludes with a booming low E. Rather than letting this ring, Eddie taps the string at the twelfth fret, creating a harmonic one octave higher, and slowly lowers the note back to its original pitch using the vibrato bar, as it simmers with feedback, like the final searing stream of lava from this volcanic instrumental.

'You Really Got Me' (Davies)
Although Van Halen had no shortage of strong original material, Templeman picked this cover of The Kinks' 1964 breakthrough hit as their first single. Its hasty release was allegedly prompted by the discovery that rival group Angel

planned to pip Van Halen to the post by rush-releasing their own rocked-up version of the song. Even so, it's a strong opening gambit; the sound of a rock 'n' roll renaissance bursting forth from a sun-soaked Pasadena backyard party, distilled into two-and-a-half minutes. Most elements of The Kinks' original version remain intact; the primitive two-chord riff, which many cite as the starting point for heavy rock and punk; the driving beat; the head-shaking 'Oh Yeeeaahh' harmonies. Nevertheless, Van Halen instil the song with their personality, making it entirely their own.

As the rising punk movement threatened rock's old guard with obsolescence, the simple, primal aggression of the riff helps to establish Van Halen as tougher, livelier and more punk-adjacent than your average late-seventies hard rockers, although Eddie's warm tone sounds less punky than Dave Davies' gnarly slashed speaker racket on the original record. Roth sings the song relatively straightforwardly, but the force of his personality makes his version entirely distinct from Ray Davies' original performance. While Davies was the slightly nerdy English boy, going wild in a hormonal frenzy, Roth radiates self-assurance and a tongue-in-cheek attitude. After the second chorus, Eddie engages his phaser and unleashes a solo. He packs a busy eight bars with Chuck Berry-style double stops, light-speed tapping and wild string bends, ending on a sustained note of feedback, creating a stuttering Morse code-like effect using his pickup selector. Roth half-croons, half-whispers the third verse over an echoing backdrop of voices gasping, cooing, squealing and sighing in apparent ecstasy across the stereo spectrum, like a miniature version of the middle section of Led Zeppelin's *Whole Lotta Love* (1969). Before this becomes too cringeworthy, we're into a final all-guns-blazing chorus with a traditional hard rock stage show ending – a series of crashes, a big chord, a last gasp of guitar shredding, then a final unison thump. As well as providing Van Halen with their first hit, this cover helped reinvigorate the commercial fortunes of The Kinks in the US, where their early career had faltered after the American Federation of Musicians banned them from performing for much of the latter half of the 1960s. Their revival was already underway by the time Van Halen arrived on the national scene, but it's notable that 1979's *Low Budget* became their highest-charting US album in the wake of the success of 'You Really Got Me'.

'Ain't Talkin' 'Bout Love' (Van Halen, Van Halen, Roth, Anthony)
Conceived as a punk parody, 'Ain't Talkin' 'Bout Love' certainly taps into the simplicity and raw energy of that genre. The chorus and main riff are built on just two chords, with a third popping up in passing during the intro and verse. Really, the band's blend of musical virtuosity and extrovert showmanship is far removed from the ultra-minimalist street-level rock of the Ramones and their ilk. Nevertheless, the track clearly resonated with at least some punks, with San Pedro art-hardcore legends The Minutemen releasing a somewhat-deconstructed cover in 1984.

The recording begins with an iconic riff – a series of palm-muted arpeggios, rounded off with a short phrase played on the lower strings. Eddie's Echoplex tape delay lends the riff a haunting quality, while an MXR flanger, kicked on for the final four notes of each repetition, creates a soaring jet-engine sound. As a build-up of tom-toms introduces the full band, Eddie abandons delicate arpeggios for crunching block chords. Mike's bass is the punkiest element present, maintaining a barrage of pummelling eighth notes worthy of Dee Dee Ramone! Dave's vocal is none too melodic, but brimming with attitude. The lyrics are dark in tone, matching the music's minor key, as Roth's tough, misanthropic narrative voice sneers out lines resembling dialogue from a hardboiled detective novel. A story is hinted at, with suggestions of drug abuse ('I've got something you *need*') and prostitution ('You're semi-good lookin', and on the streets again'), wrapped up in a bitter, loveless relationship. Roth sketches a seedy scenario from LA's sordid underworld, allowing the listener to fill in the details for themselves.

After the second chorus, Eddie plays a simple, effective melody on his B string, with the open high E ringing freely for a sitar-like drone. Perhaps inspired by the line's raga-like quality, Templeman suggested he double this line in on a Coral electric sitar. Not a true sitar, this is an electric guitar fitted with thirteen extra drone strings that vibrate in sympathy with the regular six, and a bridge which replicates the buzzing sound of sitar fretting. This is panned to the right, almost exactly doubling the solo until the very end, where the guitar line plays high, flashy hammer-ons, while the sitar moves to the lower octave. The third verse drops to an intimate murmur. Just as we're getting used to the quiet, the repeated phrase 'bleed baby' is accompanied by an aggressive accent from the band, punctuated by a blast of Eddie's flanger. The chorus is simple and powerful, with Mike's harmony a third above Dave's lead, and Eddie adding a shouted emphasis to the word 'love'. After a reiteration of the instrumental, the track closes with more repetitions of the riff, now accompanying a yobbish chant of 'Hey! Hey! Hey!' before a bombastic ending. The track was released as a single in October 1978 and is widely recognised as one of Van Halen's defining moments. Its influence spread beyond the rock world, with the opening riff sampled by Miami hip-hop collective 2 Live Crew for the very lewd 'The Fuck Shop' (1989), and given the drum & bass treatment by Liverpool-based big-beat group Apollo 440 on 1997's 'Ain't Talkin 'Bout Dub'.

'I'm The One' (Van Halen, Van Halen, Roth, Anthony)

Following that barnstormer, Van Halen somehow up the ante again on this tour de force of adrenaline-pumping rock, with their flashy musicianship, chest-beating machismo and goofy showmanship cranked to eleven! If, on tunes like 'La Grange' (1973 – regularly covered in early Van Halen live sets), ZZ Top melded John Lee Hooker's blues-boogie with hard rock power, 'I'm the One' overhauls that template, harnessing it to the virtuoso intricacy of jazz fusion. The main riff starts the track in the Billy Gibbons boogie-rock mould, albeit played at a scorching tempo, with enough scalding triplet runs and whammy bar acrobatics to scare the cowboy hat off any Texas blues purist. As a snare backbeat enters, the track feels about to kick into gear. Instead, it drops back to a solo guitar, accompanied only by hi-hat and off-beat cymbal-catch accents. These lend the track a jazzy feel, recalling the bebop practice of 'dropping bombs', pioneered by Kenny Clarke. A rattling snare fill introduces the full band, and Alex powers the track along with a double-bass shuffle – a beat made famous by fusion great, Billy Cobham on 'Quadrant 4', from his debut solo LP, *Spectrum* (1973). The use of twin bass drums was an innovation of swing legend, Louie Bellson, becoming popular with adventurous jazz-influenced rock drummers in the later sixties. Notable among these were Cream's Ginger Baker and Carmine Appice, whose early-seventies outfit Cactus recorded a blazing version of Mose Allison's 'Parchman Farm' (1970) – a major influence on Van Halen's up-tempo shuffles. Alex performs with rock power and intensity melded with jazzy flair and sophistication. Mike's bass locks tight with Alex's relentless kick, and elsewhere adds nimble 'walking' runs, playing a different note on every beat like a jazz double bassist, emphasising the 'heavy bebop' feel.

Roth's vocal surfs over the track, with vibrato-laden crooning, throaty blues hollering, he-man grunts and ecstatic whoops. The lyric finds Dave thumbing his nose at detractors and demanding adulation. 'We came here to entertain you, leaving here we aggravate you / Don't you know it means the same to me?' he asks, revelling in the discomfort his in-your-face personality can cause. The bridge, with its chromatically descending chord pattern, finds our narrator honing in on a target. However, there will be no smooth seduction. Instead, the chorus simply repeats the blunt demand to 'show your love' in bright harmonies, while Dave goads, pleads and cajoles. After an exceptionally fierce guitar solo, the clamorous noise drops, leaving just Roth's voice and Alex's swing-time hi-hat. The track suddenly becomes an *a capella* doo-wop number, with Roth joined in turn by Mike and Eddie singing nonsense syllables ('Ba-bada shooby-do-wah!') while adding layers of harmony. Just as abruptly, we're jolted into a dramatic instrumental build-up, leading to an emphatic final chorus and huge stadium rock ending. 'I'm The One' closes side one of the LP with an incredible rush of excitement, effortlessly melding disparate musical styles, and making a powerful statement of unshakeable self-belief.

'Jamie's Cryin'" (Van Halen, Van Halen, Roth, Anthony)

After all that testosterone, the band give us something more nuanced. The hard rock scene of the 1970s was hyper-masculine and often misogynistic. Van Halen were generally no exception to this, although there's a tongue-in-cheek element to Roth's lyrics that makes them seem slightly less crass to modern listeners than those of many of his contemporaries. 'Jamie's Cryin'" unusually takes the perspective of a girl – the 'Jamie' of the title – who has turned down an opportunity for a one-night stand as she questions her choices, and longs for a deeper emotional connection. The track has a mid-tempo groove, propelled by a great, thumping bass line, doubled on guitar. Eddie overdubs a high lead, full of long, lugubrious string bends and slow, sighing vibrato bar dives, foreshadowing Jamie's mood. Roth's vocal is calculatedly sleazy, teasing words into yelps and moans. Dave took care to look after himself, sleeping and eating well prior to recording the song. However, Templeman wasn't happy with the performances this healthy approach produced, and ordered Roth to eat a cheeseburger and smoke a joint before resuming recording! The first verse sets the scene vividly but economically: Jamie's partner 'wanted her tonight / and it was now or never', but she rejected his advance. The tone is ambiguous; we see the encounter from Jamie's perspective, but Roth's sarcastic 'he made her feel *so* sad' undercuts the sympathy we feel. This sardonic tone continues in the chorus, where bubblegum pop harmonies sing 'oh, oh, oh, Jamie's cryin'' in a mocking playground chant.

The second verse fleshes out the narrative, before a breezy bridge, with light, shimmering, arpeggiated chords. Alex shifts to propulsive disco-like 16ths on his hi-hat, as our heroine considers writing to the boy in question to renew contact, although, as Dave cynically observes: 'she knows what that'll get her'. The heart of the song lies in the brief middle eight. Alex drops to a gentle rumba-like rhythm while Eddie audibly rolls down the volume to play a soft minor-key accompaniment. Over lush harmonies, a surprisingly sincere Roth explains our protagonist's quandary: 'Now, Jamie's been in love before, and she knows what love is for / It should mean a little... a little more than one night stands'. It's a beautiful section, closer to something from an early Beatles record than typical hard rock. After a reiteration of the bridge, an extended out-chorus finds Eddie's intro lead returning to provide an additional harmony to the vocal. 'Jamie's Cryin'' isn't the album's best-known song, but it perfectly illustrates Van Halen's knack for building immaculate pop hooks on rock foundations, and reveals Roth to be a more sensitive, empathetic lyricist than many would credit.

'Atomic Punk' (Van Halen, Van Halen, Roth, Anthony)

We might expect a song with 'punk' in the title to musically resemble that genre. However, although it possesses punky energy and aggression, this record is stylistically closer to heavy metal – more so than the album's other tracks. Although the band's loud guitars and long hair seemed to align them with the metal genre, they were keen to distance themselves from the label, with Roth preferring the term 'big rock'. Their concise songs, unabashed pop sensibility and generally bright, buoyant tone set them apart from the denim and leather brigade. That said, 'Atomic Punk' is packed with metal's hallmarks – all razor-sharp minor key riffs and chugging power chord drive.

Roth delivers a sneeringly aggressive vocal, while Mike and Alex forsake dynamics for pedal-to-the-metal force. The sound pre-empts Iron Maiden's genre-redefining self-titled debut (1980), which featured clearly Roth-indebted vocals from original Maiden singer Paul DiAnno.

The track starts with Eddie rhythmically rubbing his palm along damped strings, processed through his Phase 90 and Echoplex, creating an effect that foreshadows the DJ scratching effects of Rage Against the Machine guitarist Tom Morello. A thumping snare fill introduces the band, and subtlety is abandoned. Roth's lyrics are even more outrageously self-aggrandising than usual. The lone outlaw portrayed elsewhere has become an awesome super-being: 'a child of the storm... ruler of these netherworlds'. Like Marvel's Bruce Banner – exposed to gamma rays to become the Incredible Hulk – our narrator is 'a victim of the science age'. It's enjoyably ridiculous, reaching a pompous peak with the chorus's proclamation: 'nobody rules these streets at night but me – the atomic punk!'. The portentous tone may betray the influence of Kim Fowley. This Sunset Strip scenester had been an early supporter of Van Halen, helping to promote them, and co-writing several songs. None of these were selected for the LP, but the language and imagery of 'Atomic Punk' contain familiar Fowley tropes. The idea of ruling the streets or commanding the dark underworld is a recurring Fowley theme – witness his 1975 album, *Animal God of the Streets* or the song 'King of the Night Time World' (1976), co-written for Kiss. 'Atomic Punk' is an entertaining blast of brute-force rock, and a bold statement of Roth's larger-than-life persona.

'Feel Your Love Tonight' (Van Halen, Van Halen, Roth, Anthony)
If 'Atomic Punk' represents Van Halen's heavier side, 'Feel Your Love Tonight' finds them at their most effervescent – an irresistible ode to libidinous youth. Roth has a knack for capturing the essence of teenage experience in a pithy, memorable string of rhyming couplets. Over three short verses, he vividly depicts an all-American Friday night out, circa 1978. This starts with a fumbled backseat seduction, which is firmly rebuffed ('I'm sorry honey if I took it just a little too far'). Undeterred, our narrator plans his post-work revelry, certain of inevitable conquest: 'We'll hit the town... by midnight I'll be flying... by morning, you'll be mine'. The lyric is a totally convincing evocation of male teen behaviour – one moment full of boorish swagger, the next awkward, fumbling and apologetic and finally, in the bridge, insecure and pleading ('I'm beggin' on my bended knees').

Musically, it's upbeat and hooky, with few hard edges. There's a classic rock n' roll-sounding riff in E, breezy open chords under the verses, and a tense plummet to C for the bridge, with great vocal interplay. This culminates in a cliffhanging pause on B, as the narrator anxiously awaits the answer to his pleas before resolving to E for the chorus. The first chorus is just a single, 'I can't wait to feel your love tonight', followed by a Beatles/Little Richard-ish 'whoooo!'. The second is differently arranged, with the rhythm section dropping out and the backing vocals harmonising answering phrases to Dave's lead over muted chords. Eddie's blazing solo is accompanied by an overdubbed rhythm guitar and handclaps, which provide a classic sixties pop feel. The solo lands back on the expectant B chord, the tension heightened by a swooping bass fill. The extended out-chorus begins stripped down to just vocals. The guitar and rhythm section join in turn, gradually building. Just as the song has got back into gear, the instruments suddenly drop out, with the final line sung in *a capella* harmony. The song's delivery rocks hard, but the building blocks are pure bubblegum – more Bay City Rollers than Black Sabbath. It's a blend imitated by legions of (usually vastly inferior) pop-metal bands throughout the 1980s. 'Feel Your Love Tonight' was released as the B-side of 'Ain't Talkin' 'Bout Love' but could easily have been a hit in its own right.

'Little Dreamer' (Van Halen, Van Halen, Roth, Anthony)

'Little Dreamer' provides further evidence of Van Halen's remarkable versatility, featuring a sultry R&B-tinged groove, far removed from their usual flashy exuberance. It slinks along on a bluesy minor 7th riff, with the guitar dropping to a barely-audible root note chug during the verses, and the rhythm section staying 'in the pocket'. Eddie's lead breaks and solo are lyrical rather than explosive, and Roth's vocal is smoky and soulful, demonstrating that, behind the posturing, he can really *sing*. The track is a significant improvement on the version recorded for the 1977 demo, on which both lyrics and melody seem vague, as though still works in progress. The demo is also faster and more aggressive – closer to bog-standard hard-rock than the slow-burning melancholic gem it eventually became. The lyrics address the titular 'little dreamer' – an ambitious kid, who dreamt big, even as cruel peers voted them 'least likely to succeed'. While the first verse stays in the moody minor key, the second segues into a major key bridge, as the narrative moves from past to present. Now the 'dreamer' is successful, and 'no-one's talking 'bout those crazy days gone past'. The simple chorus is made atmospheric by superb falsetto harmony backing vocals. The final double chorus sees the brothers letting off some steam after a restrained performance. The band comes to a sudden halt while Roth delivers the melismatic final line solo before the track ends with a soft cymbal swell and a low moan of feedback.

For a notoriously brash, over-the-top band, 'Little Dreamer' is remarkably thoughtful and subtle. Dave often portrays himself as the tough outsider, but this track reveals his more vulnerable side. The 'dreamer' could be a younger Roth – the ostracised schoolchild, the wannabe singer who no one thought was good enough. Now, on the cusp of success, he can reflect on hard times while basking in triumph. *Little Dreamer* isn't one of the band's more high-profile tracks, but shows surprising depth, and remains a favourite among hardcore fans.

'Ice Cream Man' (Brim)

The album's second cover was written and recorded in 1953 by John Brim, a singer/guitarist from the thriving 1950s Chicago blues scene. His few records met with little success, and he returned to relative obscurity until Van Halen's cover thrust his song back into the spotlight. According to Greg Renoff in *Van Halen Rising*, Dave heard the song from a friend who, fittingly, had been introduced to it by Tommy Lake, a fixture of Pasadena's party circuit who sold beer from an ice cream truck.

The track begins intimately, with a lone Roth accompanying himself on acoustic guitar. It has a live feel, including muttered asides to the 'audience' ('dedicate one to the ladies...'). Roth croons, growls and mumbles through the three verses, chorus and bridge alone. He sets a brisker pace than Brim's easy shuffle, but the delivery is light, with Dave teasing out the innuendo-laden lyrics. There's a tradition of double entendre in blues songs, and this has plenty: 'all my flavours are guaranteed to satisfy... If you let me cool you one time, you'll be my regular stop' etc. Roth also adds a line about 'pudding pie banana', just to clarify the 'flavour' he's offering! Before the second bridge, a cry of 'alright boys!' introduces the band, transforming the track into a boogie-rock rave-up. Eddie's solo is spectacular, commencing with a two-handed tapping run that zips across the fretboard from high to low before settling into wild, scattershot blues. After another chorus, rendered in three-part harmony, an overdubbed guitar trades call-and-response lines with Roth. Finally, the band slams to a halt for Dave's final elaborate *cadenza*, before a blow-out ending. It's great fun, and a first taste of the left-of-centre material that Dave brought to the band. Chicago blues purists may not applaud such irreverent treatment of a lost classic. However, the cover helped raise awareness of Brim, who enjoyed a revival in its wake, playing larger shows, and recording again for the first time in decades

'On Fire' (Van Halen, Van Halen, Roth, Anthony)

The album finishes with a song that encapsulates the band's staggering musical power and invincible self-belief. The narrator is omnipotent, invading the ears, beds and minds of the masses through music, while the bridge finds him 'hanging ten as I ride your sonic wave' – likening the adrenalised rush of the music to that felt by a surfer, poised at the crest of a wave. A crashing introductory riff gives way to a guitar rhythm of choked strings and muffled harmonics, sounding like the starter motor of a car during ignition. The song lurches into gear, with a hard-driving riff, and guttural, aggressive lead vocal. Under the verse, Eddie plays a muted low-E chug, punctuated by ascending and descending fretboard slides. A very similar riff underpins 'Negative Creep', from Nirvana's 1989 debut, *Bleach*, which may or may not be a coincidence.

After a cry of 'good god, y'all!' (cribbed from Edwin Starr's 'War' (1970)) the chorus finds Roth and Anthony shrieking, 'I'm on fire!'. Anthony plays high hammer-ons while Eddie hits a series of chords, his Echoplex's delay synchronised with Alex's kick and snare. A sinister-sounding section follows, with a low single-note riff that sounds like an amped-up spy movie theme, while ghostly, reverberating voices wail 'fire!'. Eddie's fierce solo eschews tapping for an elaborate, bubbling stream of precisely picked palm-muted triplets. The song ends with Dave whooping up a storm over the repeating chorus as the track fades. On the demo, he interjects a ridiculous growling bass 'fie-yuh!', which wisely isn't recreated here! The track is obnoxious and subtlety-free – the sound of a band revelling in their own astonishing power – a perfect way to conclude arguably the greatest debut in US rock history.

Van Halen II (1979)

Personnel:
David Lee Roth: lead vocals
Edward Van Halen: guitar, backing vocals
Michael Anthony: bass, backing vocals
Alex Van Halen: drums
Recorded at Sunset Sound Recorders, Hollywood, December 1978
Produced by Ted Templeman
Engineered by Donn Landee
Record label: Warner Brothers
Release date: 23 March 1979
Highest chart position: US: 6, UK: 23
Running time: 31.36
Current edition: 2019 reissue

Van Halen's unstoppable momentum carried them straight from recording their landmark debut, through a year of touring the world, and back into the studio with barely a chance to draw breath. Luckily, they had a cache of excellent unused songs to draw from and had been honed into an even tighter musical unit on the road, so were well prepared when summoned back to Sunset Sound in December 1978. Again, Templeman and Landee oversaw proceedings, recording the basic tracks live, and using even fewer guitar overdubs this time around. Most tracks were recorded in just six days, with only Eddie's acoustic showcase 'Spanish Fly' being added as an afterthought, and the completed album cost less to make than their debut. Although *Van Halen II* picks up where the debut left off, the band weren't resting on their laurels. This sophomore effort sees them stretching out, developing in directions hinted at on the previous album with a confidence and easy spontaneity born of newfound success and hard-earned experience. Some consider the album relatively light and poppy compared to *Van Halen*, but for me, it strikes a perfect balance between radio-friendly fun and more intense, aggressive material. Speaking to Brad Tolinski and Chris Gill in their excellent book, *Eruption*, Eddie concurred: 'I hate when albums are happy-happy or heavy-heavy all the way through. We had a little bit of both on *Van Halen II*'

The cover is simple and striking, featuring a metallic VH logo on a field of dark blue, tinged with red and orange, as though reflecting flames from below. The rear cover shows the band in posed action shots, with Eddie brandishing a new custom Charvel 'superstrat', nicknamed 'bumblebee' for its yellow and black striped finish. Roth is shown performing a leaping split, and apparently broke his ankle upon landing! Although the flared trousers place the band firmly in the seventies, their bright, colourful attire and energetic presentation are a marked contrast to the self-conscious seriousness and artistic pretensions of much of the era's rock, anticipating the flamboyance of the glam-metal bands that emerged from the LA scene in their wake.

Contemporary reviews, while generally erring on the positive side, showed critics were still too cool to fully back an act so unashamedly, unambiguously entertaining. Nevertheless, fans lapped up the record, with hit single *Dance the Night Away* helping to attract a new, more pop-oriented following. The album comfortably outsold its predecessor, going platinum within a year of release, and is one of the band's finest achievements.

'You're No Good' (Ballard)

This Clint Ballard Jr composition had been a hit several times on both sides of the Atlantic by the time Van Halen recorded it. Originally cut by R&B singer Dee Dee Warwick in 1963, Betty Everett's more sophisticated arrangement was a hit later that year. Merseybeat combo The Swinging Blue Jeans had UK success with the song in 1964 – the first version by a guitar-based rock band. The most successful recording was Linda Ronstadt's smooth soft-rock interpretation, a *Billboard* number one in 1974. The song's popularity earned it a place in Van Halen's early top 40 covers sets, and they decided to revive it to open their sophomore album. This was probably suggested by Templeman, hoping to recapture the success of 'You Really Got Me' with another reinterpreted classic. In *Eruption*, Eddie recalls:

> When we were playing the clubs, we used to do a version that sounded more like Linda Ronstadt's version, but when we had the idea to do it in the studio, I couldn't really remember how it went, so I just started noodling and that's what came out

Eddie's sketchy memory was a blessing in disguise, as the new arrangement enlivens what was already, by 1978, a well-worn oldie. Van Halen turn it into a menacing slow burn, building from an eerie, atmospheric opening to an aggressive heavy rock strut.

It opens with solo bass, treated with a flanger. Alex keeps time softly while Eddie uses his volume control to gently swell chords, muting their initial attack – a trick later used to more elaborate effect on 'Cathedral'. Incidentally, this intro was transplanted from an early Van Halen original, 'Down in Flames', which later resurfaced as the basis for 'Tattoo'. A tom-tom build-up introduces a muted, moody blues-rock riff, bearing no resemblance to Ronstadt's, or indeed any other version of the song. Roth's vocal has a loose relationship with the original melody, but his smoky, soul-influenced tones are closer to the song's R&B roots than, say, The Swinging Blue Jeans' chirpy, very-English interpretation. The major key bridge features the band's Beach Boys-like harmonies over warm, ringing arpeggios. Roth's falsetto scream brings in the chorus, accompanied by a much raunchier riff. This leaps from snarling mid-range chords to high string bends, played in unison with Roth's vocal hook, while the actual chorus is carried by the backing vocals. Eddie's solo builds from stark, yowling string bends and stuttering staccato notes to a lushly-melodic blur of tapped arpeggios and fluid legato runs. The intro's haunting chord swells reappear, as Roth, acting the scorned lover, murmurs, 'used to be I couldn't sleep at night, baby. Now you go and do what you want to'. After one more chorus, an overdubbed guitar doubles the main track's power chords and adds a closing harmony line, recalling the duelling guitars of Thin Lizzy. This unexpected take on an overplayed song is a testament to Van Halen's ability to make almost any material their own. It's not as commercial as Templeman may have hoped but it's a striking, surprisingly dark album opener.

'Dance The Night Away' (Van Halen, Van Halen, Roth, Anthony)

If Van Halen flirted with bubblegum pop with 'Jamie's Cryin'', they fully embraced it on 'Dance the Night Away'. Built on a hip-swinging calypso rhythm and simple four-chord structure, this infectious ode to the joy of youthful abandon showed that the band didn't need to rely on reimagined oldies for a hit. It skilfully melds the clobbering rhythm section and blazing guitars of hard rock with the easily relatable lyrics, hummable melody, irresistible hooks and danceable beat of the finest commercial pop. The song opens with a syncopated calypso rhythm, played on maracas and cowbell – the band's first notable recorded use of additional percussion. Eddie plays a catchy, upbeat riff, based on major triads rather than typical heavy rock 'power chords' (which use only the root note and fifth, without the emotional colour provided by a dark minor or bright major third). His 'brown sound' has never sounded warmer, setting the song's ebullient tone. Roth matches this with a vibrant vocal – melodic, but packed with characterful off-the-cuff touches, like the whooping leap in pitch on the second syllable of the phrase 'across the room', followed by a barely suppressed chuckle, as though surprised by his own vocal gymnastics. From the opening 'have you seen her?', the verses make us confident to Roth's narrator as he admires a young dancing girl. The bridge begins with a one-beat rest – a moment's uncertain hesitation before the narrator directly addresses the girl: 'Ooh, baby baby, wontcha turn your head my way?'. This imploring moment is lent weight by the addition of backing vocals, a plunge to the serious-sounding relative minor and a dramatic dynamic build-up. The chorus breaks the tension, returning to the major key with sunny three-part harmonies. As the signature riff plays in the left channel, Eddie overdubs a new countermelody, played entirely in tapped harmonics. This tricky technique involves fretting notes with the left hand and using the right to tap the string exactly 12 frets higher, creating a pure, ringing tone.

A second chorus leads into an instrumental, which oscillates between B sus. 5th and A with an augmented 3rd, the ringing suspended notes creating a yearning quality. This returns us to the calypso-flavoured intro, now played an octave higher on phased tapped harmonics, with an almost steel drum-like timbre. After a crescendo, we conclude with an extended chorus and slow fade. The only song (aside from the instrumental 'Spanish Fly') to be written entirely during the album sessions, 'Dance the Night Away' is three minutes of pure joy. Released as a single in April 1979, it was the band's first top 20 hit, reaching number 15 on the *Billboard* chart. It remains one of their best-loved songs, and its blend of rock power and pop melody has been oft-imitated but never equalled.

'Somebody Get Me A Doctor' (Van Halen, Van Halen, Roth, Anthony)

After that pop moment, it's time for something obnoxiously aggressive! A gloriously unsubtle hymn to excessive cocaine use, this song was a live favourite, appearing on both the Gene Simmons and Warner Bros. demos. While many elements remain unchanged from earlier versions, this new recording features a fresh, more dramatic introduction, and simplified, more coherent lyrics. While the song originally started in tempo, over a regular drumbeat, this arrangement commences with declamatory chords, interspersed with thudding tom-toms. As the last chord rings, an off-mic count-in introduces a particularly mean-sounding riff, accompanied by hi-hat 16ths. The riff's actual notes are standard rock fare; the attitude comes from Eddie's articulation, with snarling slides, spluttering palm-muted strings and a hint of venomous vibrato.

The verse riff alternates between E and F chords over an E bass pedal, creating an uneasy discord reflected in Roth's tumultuous lyrics. While cocaine isn't specifically mentioned, there are clues to the cause of our narrator's medical emergency, with suggestions of chemically-induced numbness ('Feelin' *no* pain') and references to 'speedin' down that line'. The chorus consists of the title sung over the main riff, once in thuggish-sounding unison, and again with Mike's high harmony bringing pop polish to this otherwise raw, nasty track. After the third verse, Eddie belts out a fiery blues riff, interspersed with ominous volume swells over a stop-time rhythm. This develops into a solo, played over a new chord sequence. Building from zippy tremolo picking to an intricate, muted melodic line, decorated with piercing showers of harmonics, the solo is accompanied by loose-limbed drums and nimble, muscular bass. The track pauses on a ringing chord, with Roth leading some impromptu applause, before we're plunged back into the riff, followed by a final verse and chorus. As the last chords approach, Roth delivers the punchline: 'somebody give me a shot!' – his solution to chemical excess is more pharmaceuticals! It's easy to see why 'Somebody Get Me a Doctor' was an early concert staple. It's totally ridiculous, celebrating a numbskull lifestyle that was already clichéd by the time Van Halen hit Sunset Strip. It's also outrageously good fun, rocking so hard that, by the end of its 2:53 run-time, you're guaranteed to have a big dumb grin on your face.

'Bottoms Up!' (Van Halen, Van Halen, Roth, Anthony)

This barnstormer appeared in the band's repertoire after the debut album, but in time to become the regular encore of their 1978 tour. In the mould of 'I'm the One', although with a *slightly* less hectic tempo, 'Bottoms Up' utilises Alex's double-bass shuffle to propel a Cactus/ZZ Top-style riff. The track starts with a brief, hushed intro, based around a softly-picked blues riff. However, any expectation of a quiet, laid-back listen is abruptly shattered by a thunderous drum fill, and the song takes off at a gallop. The lyrics are a simple paean to two of Roth's passions: booze and pretty women. The unsubtle *double entendre* of the 'Oh, oh baby, bottoms up!' chorus is entirely intentional! The verse maintains the amped-up boogie feel, but the bridge takes a jazzier turn with a lurching chromatic descent. Alex throws in some wildly syncopated accents before slipping neatly back into the groove for the chorus. Anthony's harmony adds pop sparkle to the 'oh, oh baby', while 'bottoms up!' is bellowed in throaty unison, emphasising the deliberate crudity. After a second verse, Eddie overdubs a tasty solo, while the main guitar track keeps grinding out the riff. The bluesy guitar from the intro now provides the backing for a vocal breakdown, with the tipsy-sounding band audibly struggling to keep straight faces while singing 'come um um um um um baby, bottoms up'. The beery bonhomie is interrupted by a gigantic drum fill which returns us to the main riff, and a second, even tastier overdubbed solo, followed by a crashing conclusion. It's hardly the most thought-provoking number, but captures the hyperactive, woozy spirit of the era perfectly. Also, as the second consecutive celebration of rock n' roll debauchery on this record, it sees the band well on their way to establishing a justly deserved reputation as rock's premier party animals.

'Outta Love Again' (Van Halen, Van Halen, Roth, Anthony)

Alex excels here with a staggering blend of jazz-funk finesse and explosive power. The song is funkier than anything the band had recorded to this point, with Eddie noting in *Eruption* its similarity to 'What is Hip?' from Tower of Power's eponymous 1973 LP. That track is more relaxed than 'Outta Love Again', but features a similar bassline – a constant, tense throb of root-note 16ths, rather than the spare syncopation of most seventies funk. Over this urgent groove, Eddie plays a terse, snarling riff, the notes wrung angrily from the guitar and abruptly choked off. The dynamics echo Roth's lyrics, which describe trouble brewing in a relationship through the simmering, anxious verses. This boils over into a blazing argument in the bridge, represented by lurching runs of chromatically ascending chords and wild, elastic drum fills. The perfunctory lyrics are elevated by a grandstanding performance from Roth. His voice becomes another percussion instrument, delivering bursts of machine-gun syllables like verbal drum rolls, or slurring across the beat with lazy, jazzy phrasing. Backing vocals bring cohesion to the chorus behind Dave's shrieks and growls, and add pop zing to the second and third verses, chiming in with a harmonised 'didn't you?' after each accusatory line.

After each of the first two choruses, there's an instrumental. The first finds Eddie wrenching strangulated pinched harmonics from his guitar. The second, a more conventional solo, highlights the incredible polyrhythmic interplay between the two brothers – an almost psychic bond, impossible for most musicians to replicate. The song was one of the band's earliest, dating back to the Mark Stone era. It had fallen out of regular setlist rotation until revived for the album, and was rarely played again after 1979. Nevertheless, it's a tremendous recording, capturing the lightning-in-a-bottle chemistry of an untouchable band at their peak.

'Light Up the Sky' (Van Halen, Van Halen, Roth, Anthony)

Side two begins with this exciting, challenging track: a freewheeling hymn to the explosive creative potential of the young generation. A dizzying, disorienting intro sees Eddie playing a rapidly rising chromatic figure while Mike's bassline descends in pitch simultaneously before launching into a chugging, aggressive riff. Dave maintains the intensity, delivering rapid-fire lyrics across two separate tracks, allowing him to overlap lines without pausing for breath. An anonymous article on the *Van Halen News Desk* website speculates that Roth's lyrics were inspired by a passage from Kerouac's *On the Road* (1957), praising the 'mad ones' who 'burn burn burn, like fabulous yellow Roman candles'. While there's no concrete evidence to corroborate this theory, the passage does align with the theme of 'Light up the Sky'. The well-read singer is likely to have been familiar with *On the Road,* and even if the book wasn't a direct influence, there's a Kerouac-like energy and vibrancy to the lyrics: 'We're all bad breakers coming out of the gate/ Takin' chances with a crash and burn'. The actual lyric could be 'we're the crash and burn'; no Roth-era Van Halen LP came with a lyric sheet, so the exact wording of many early songs is up for debate. This ambiguity was deliberate, as Dave explains in his book:

> Some of this is meant to be rhythmic, sometimes it was attitude, which revved up so hard it just defies lyrics, no certain string of words can approximate those syllables.

The attitude is revved hard throughout the verses of 'Light Up the Sky', which depict reckless youth, rising above and beyond a scared, confused older generation. The bridge finds our narrator receiving a mysterious summons – initially through his television, and later in a 'crazy vision' – voiced by Eddie and Mike, singing 'open your eyes, leave it all behind'. After a second bridge, the music suddenly calms. Eddie's warm, phase-shifted guitar plays a high, muted major-key rhythm part, while Dave's husky falsetto sings a lullaby-like refrain. Just as suddenly, the calm is shattered by a scream of 'light up!', and Eddie launches into an incendiary solo, with strafing bursts of machine-gun tremolo picking and dizzying vibrato bar swoops. Alex takes a rare solo, starting simply on kick, snare and hats, then gradually twisting the song's rhythm into knots while introducing more toms and cymbals. Bass and guitar creep back in, and a series of juddering triplet flams heralds the outro, which is the song's true chorus. With the band blazing at full throttle, Dave and Mike harmonise on the song's title, their voices treated with ghostly reverse echo. As Eddie's overdubbed lead brings the track to a dramatic climax, Dave unleashes a final scream of 'light 'em up!'. 'Light Up the Sky' is not one of the band's most widely known songs, nor does it feature on their 'best of' compilations or official live releases. Nevertheless, it's a favourite of many hardcore fans (this author included), and, according to an interview in *Eruption*, was Eddie's favourite track on *Van Halen II*. It's a magical blend of progressive, cerebral ideas and spur-of-the-moment adrenaline – almost a hybrid of the intricate heavy prog of Canada's cult heroes, Rush, and the speed-freak aggression of hardcore punk, with a smattering of beat generation motormouth jive sprinkled over the top. A heady blend, indeed!

'Spanish Fly' (Van Halen, Van Halen, Roth, Anthony)

Rather than duplicating 'Eruption' with another blazing electric guitar showcase, 'Spanish Fly' highlights an altogether softer, although no less spectacular side to Eddie's playing. Attending Templeman's 1978 New Year's Eve party, Eddie – ill-at-ease in social gatherings – retreated to a corner to noodle on an acoustic guitar he found there. Hearing this, Templeman was astonished to discover Eddie's playing was just as acrobatic and fluid on a wide-necked acoustic as on his hot-rodded electric. Eddie purchased a nylon-strung Ovation, and soon afterwards, 'Spanish Fly' was recorded. The Spanish fly is a beetle that secretes the poisonous compound *cantharidin*, traditionally considered an aphrodisiac. Nylon-strung guitars are also known as Spanish guitars, so the title could also refer to Eddie's soaring performance on the instrument! Beginning with delicate tapped harmonics (tricky on an overdriven electric, trickier on acoustic guitar), the piece gathers pace, with bursts of two-handed tapping, speedy alternate picking and chiming natural harmonics. The track peaks with a disarmingly beautiful passage of rippling, harp-like two-handed arpeggios. The tapping slows on an A7 arpeggio, leading back to the chord of D sus4, played again with tapped harmonics. 'Spanish Fly' is only a brief interlude, but this ethereal, harmonically sophisticated piece reveals the depth of Eddie's talent as a composer and guitarist. Some envious fellow guitarists have tried to dismiss his electric prowess as mere party tricks. Hearing him play on an acoustic instrument without amplification or effects, his mastery of the instrument and jaw-dropping inventiveness are undeniable.

'D.O.A' (Van Halen, Van Halen, Roth, Anthony)

Following that delicate interlude, 'D.O.A' is emphatically loud and crude. After the opening chord emerges from dive-bombed dissonance, a pick slide introduces a brilliantly blunt one-bar riff. This repeats throughout most of the track, with the rhythm section creating the underlying harmonic movement, and alternating between pounding out solid eighth notes or locking tight with the guitar. The effect is punky and swaggering, bristling with an obnoxious attitude that is reflected in Roth's lyrics. The song was recorded for the 1977 demo, but the original lyrics were a shambles – unclear, repetitive and nonsensical. By *Van Halen II*, the narrative has come together, depicting a scenario similar to *The Wild One* (Laslzo Benedek, 1953), the noir/exploitation classic, in which a Marlon Brando-led outlaw motorcycle gang runs afoul of a small town's establishment. Our narrator and his cohort roll into town, 'broke and hungry'. Fearful locals send first the sheriff and then the mayor 'to try and drive us away', with our protagonist eventually facing trial for an unspecified offence. Roth has fun creating a guttural voice for the foreman of the jury's verdict: 'outta luck!', recalling the father, boss and congressman in Eddie Cochran's 1958 hit 'Summertime Blues' ('you can't use the car 'cos you didn't work a lick'). A version of that song, based on The Who's *Live At Leeds* rendition, had been a fixture of early Van Halen sets, and probably influenced Dave here. There's a hint of peril in the minor-key bridge as Roth wails 'And I'm alone on the highway, wanted…'. However, as the chorus begins with the words '…dead or alive', the band's Beach Boys-like harmonies restore a bright, sunny tone. In fact, although dealing with edgy subject matter, the whole song is upbeat and breezy, with a catchy major-key melody, and lyrics that offset their darker content with humour. After a couple of wild, whammy bar-abusing lead breaks, the track slowly fades, Roth narrating as the outlaws accelerate into the distance ('I'm a spark on the horizon'). Late in the fade, the rhythm breaks down, replaced by stabbing chords, interspersed with percussive chugging; it sounds like our protagonist has stalled, and is frantically trying to restart his engine – a final punchline to this hugely enjoyable blast of bold, snotty rock.

'Women In Love…' (Van Halen, Van Halen, Roth, Anthony)

This intriguing song has its origins in 'Woman in Love', which appeared on both the Gene Simmons and Warner Bros. demos. However, aside from the basic subject matter and similar title, nothing from the original song remains. 'Woman in Love' was an up-tempo rocker, with lyrics depicting their narrator discovering his girlfriend having an affair with another woman. The song wasn't totally without merit, but with crass lyrics, and few hooks, it didn't make the cut for the debut. 'Women in Love' is a different beast entirely. The subject matter remains the same but is handled with more sophistication. The narrator now directly addresses his girlfriend, putting the listener in the centre of the breakup. While the original song builds to a shock reveal of the girl's bisexuality, the revised version is framed as a universal break-up song, with only the last line of the second verse ('Honey, if you're needin' a woman just as bad as me, you ought to be going') revealing the twist to careful listeners. Roth, a voracious reader, may have taken inspiration from D.H Lawrence's 1920 novel of the same title, with its undertones of bisexual longing. However, there is another, more prosaic possible source of inspiration: an identically named forum in *Penthouse* magazine, which invited female readers to share their sexual experiences.

The original's lively-but-generic strut has been replaced by some of Van Halen's most evocative music, starting with a beautiful, glistening guitar intro, the first part of which is played almost entirely on tapped harmonics. The sparkling clean tone, thickened by double-tracking, sounds more like an electric piano than guitar. A drum fill introduces a melodic, melancholic riff, under which Mike maintains a staccato pedal-note pulse, adding tasteful melodic touches after each phrase. Dave's vocal sounds unusually tender and vulnerable, lending lines like 'It seems like loving you is just a crazy dream' a pleading fragility, far from his usual alpha-male ultra-confidence. A more strident tone emerges in the bridge, with Mike's high tenor bolstering Roth's lead, and adding a harmony to the end of each line. The main riff returns for the chorus, now with vocal harmonies providing answering phrases to Dave's lead. Eschewing pyrotechnics, Eddie's solo shows tasteful restraint, playing a simple melodic line, decorated with fluttering trills. After another bridge and chorus, there's a dark, foreboding outro. Eddie plays slashing power chords on his lower strings, while his open higher strings provide a drone. Dave unleashes a frenzy of moans, grunts and yelps, ending on a trademark two-tone scream. It's a sonically-rich song of surprising emotional depth, showing how rapidly Van Halen's craft had matured in just two years.

'Beautiful Girls' (Van Halen, Van Halen, Roth, Anthony)

Wet T-shirt nights were an entertainment staple of many Sunset Strip clubs in the 1970s, including Gazzarri's, where Van Halen had a long residency prior to getting signed. During such contests, they were required to provide a raunchy bump-and-grind rhythm to set the mood, and it was for this purpose that they wrote 'Bring on the Girls', a track recorded for the 1977 demo. Initially considered too crude, the lyrics were tweaked, and the song – now retitled 'Beautiful Girls' – was picked to close *Van Halen II*. The song takes us to the beach, where our narrator, looking for love, spies a likely target: 'she had a drink in her hand, she had her toes in the sand, and whoah! What a beautiful girl!'. He rhapsodises in entertaining patter, packed with clever internal rhymes and not-so-subtle innuendo. The accompaniment blends ZZ Top-like deep-fried boogie with loose, hip-swinging funk. Eddie and Mike trade riffs, before Alex establishes a steady groove, with a syncopated push to the first beat of each bar. The track gathers momentum, peaking with the stomping chorus, as Mike and Eddie add gleaming harmonies, and a hearty bellow of 'ah yeah, beautiful girls!'. The second verse finds our narrator making a bold if clumsy attempt at seduction. After a brief, blazing guitar solo, we catch up with our protagonist. Now, he's 'seaside sittin', just smokin' and drinkin'' like the girl in the first verse. The girl, of course, is long gone, but our hero is undeterred and ready to renew the hunt. In an extended out-chorus, the backing vocals repeat the refrain while Dave enacts another failed seduction attempt ('What's your name, honey? Hey! Where you goin'?'). A huge drum fill leads to a dead stop, and Dave ends the record with a big sloppy kiss. The song encapsulates Van Halen's party spirit, and helped to crystallise Roth's public persona: overbearing and cocky, but also charming and self-deprecating. He doesn't just sing the song, he *acts* it, and for all its undeniable sexism, the track still comes across as harmless knockabout fun – nowhere near as crass as later songs it undoubtedly inspired, such as Motley Crue's 'Girls, Girls, Girls' (1987). Released as a single in August 1979, it only reached number 84 in the US charts but has remained a fan favourite, appearing on setlists throughout the Roth era.

Women And Children First (1980)

Personnel:
David Lee Roth: lead vocals, acoustic guitar on 'Could This Be Magic?'
Edward Van Halen: guitar, electric piano, backing vocals
Michael Anthony: bass, backing vocals
Alex Van Halen: drums
Additional personnel:
Nicolette Larson: backing vocals on 'Could This Be Magic?'
Recorded at Sunset Sound Recorders, Hollywood, December 1979 – February 1980
Produced by Ted Templeman
Engineered by Donn Landee
Record label: Warner Brothers
Release date: 26 March, 1980
Highest chart position: US: 6, UK: 15
Running time: 33:35
Current edition: 2019 reissue

As the 1980s approached, Van Halen's momentum was unstoppable. No sooner had the band returned from touring *Van Halen II*, than they were back in Sunset Sound to cut a follow-up, albeit with a brief pause to renegotiate their record contract, their runaway success having substantially increased their bargaining power. Sticking with the approach that worked so well on the first two albums, the band flew through recording with the instrumental tracks all completed within four days and the whole process boxed off within two weeks. While Roth and Templeman liked to include recognisable cover songs on the group's albums, Edward was reluctant to rely on other people's compositions. Accordingly, *Women and Children First* became the first Van Halen LP to feature entirely original songs, some written especially for the album, and some reworked from material dating back to the band's earliest demos.

The album's cover featured a black-and-white shot of the band huddled around Eddie, who is playing a distinctive guitar. This instrument, nicknamed 'the shark', began life as an Ibanez Destroyer, and was one of Eddie's main guitars, played extensively on the first two albums. In a fit of creativity, Eddie decided to make the instrument more unique by attacking it with a chainsaw! This ruined the guitar's tone but did at least create a cool focal point for an album cover. Although the band look like they're having a blast, the monochrome photos and sombre colour scheme reflect the darker tone creeping into Van Halen's music. Although there's still plenty of party spirit in tracks like 'Everybody Wants Some!' and 'Romeo Delight', the band's pop sensibility has taken a back seat. In his thoughtful examination of the band's underlying philosophy, *Van Halen: Exuberant California Zen Rock 'N Roll*, John Scanlan describes *Women and Children First* as 'perhaps their loosest, most underrated album... in tune with a rawer, more vicious kind of attitude'. It might have made more commercial sense to make an album full of 'Dance the Night Away' and 'You Really Got Me' clones. However, with the seventies rock's old guard being succeeded by a generation of tough, street-level metal acts, and LA punk splintering into the hyper-aggressive hardcore scene, and a parallel wave of raw roots-rock bands, this fierce, punchy 33-minute blast captured the zeitgeist perfectly.

The album did little to change the critics' love-hate relationship with Van Halen, although David Fricke in *Rolling Stone* managed to find some positives behind the usual disclaimers:

Megalomania of this kind is an acquired taste, yet the haste with which *Women and Children First* bullied its way into the Top Ten suggests there's a little Van Halen in everybody.

For me, the album falls into a valley between the catchy party-rock of its predecessor and the dark experimentation of *Fair Warning*, without quite matching the peaks of either. Nevertheless, it's their hardest-rocking LP and a wild, exhilarating listening experience that still sounds as fresh and vital today as it did over 40 years ago.

'And The Cradle Will Rock...' (Van Halen, Van Halen, Roth, Anthony)

Perversely, Van Halen's hardest-hitting LP starts with ultra-heavy... keyboards? Yes, although the riff driving 'And The Cradle Will Rock' has the familiar 'brown sound', it's performed on a Wurlitzer electric piano, played through Eddie's Marshall stack and pedal board for a guitar-like tone (the same trick Deep Purple's Jon Lord used for his signature Hammond organ sound). For the introductory sound effect, Edward hammered the low keys of the Wurlitzer (breaking one in the process!), feeding the resulting noise through a flanger. A sturdy mid-tempo beat backs the minor-key piano riff, while a guitar overdub adds an atmospheric single-note drone. The major-key verses brighten the weighty, dark sound, while Dave exposes an inter-generational rift. Whereas 'Light Up the Sky' showed a vibrant younger generation intimidating their elders with explosive potential, 'And the Cradle Will Rock' takes a more cynical view of the generation gap. Here, parents find it 'kinda frightening how this younger generation swings', not because of their creative spontaneity, but due to old-fashioned juvenile delinquency. Roth's lyrics chart the fall of a youngster who starts by staying up late and ends up homeless and unemployed. However, if the verses show sympathy for concerned parents, the chorus embraces the chaos: 'the cradle will rock... and I say rock on!'.

The guitar stays low-key, only coming to the fore after the second chorus. Eddie's solo is split into two parts, with the first played on a semi-hollow

Gibson ES-335 for a mellower-than-usual tone. This starts with a brilliant flurry of tapping, wailing bends and light-speed picking, before dropping to a whisper as Roth's concerned parent enquires, 'have you seen junior's grades?'. As the band comes back in, another guitar takes over, a more aggressive tone powering its Chuck Berry-ish double stops and snarling blues licks. The final chorus extends to a fade-out, with guitar doubling the crunching piano chords, while Roth bellows 'rock on!'. It's an unusual but powerful opener, and a foretaste of the mean, moody sounds to come on the band's next LP. Released as the sole single from *Women and Children First*, the song did not chart but became a live favourite, with Mike taking over keyboard duties onstage.

'Everybody Wants Some!' (Van Halen, Van Halen, Roth, Anthony)

Van Halen's party spirit returns with a vengeance on 'Everybody Wants Some!'. It's musically simple, with the riff, and indeed almost the entire song created around just three chords, and Roth's vocal line mostly built from just three notes. There are no pop melodies, but the abundant attitude and exuberance give this crude material incredible vitality. The track begins with an evocative tribal tom-tom beat, while Dave and Eddie conjure a menagerie of exotic animal sounds; Roth mimicking chattering primates and squawking bird calls, while Edward interjects howls of feedback and sinister string scrapes. Some huge chords blast through the tropical ambience before the full band rampages out of the jungle, with a riff that sounds like a looser, lattler AC/DC. Alex adds a little swing to the pummelling insistency with his syncopated snare accents. The tribal rhythm returns for the verse as Eddie's guitar gurgles away with a divebomb, and Dave bursts in vigorously enough to audibly overload the desk. It's a wild performance, valuing attitude over minor considerations like pitch and intelligibility. Verse two has some entertainingly nonsensical scatting to cover up a fudged lyric. In *Crazy from the Heat*, Roth explains:

> I think the original lyric was 'I've seen a lot of people just lookin' for a moonbeam'. That doesn't sizzle and snap, crackle and pop for you like going, 'Sheepa latta peepa dabba looka foh a moonbeam'...

The vocal certainly crackles with energy. Meanwhile, the lyrics – when intelligible – function on a couple of levels. There's the coarse, sexual surface meaning, bolstered by Dave's lascivious mid-song monologue ('I like the way that line runs up the back of your stockings...'). However, there's also a meditation on ambition and desire, and the need to actively pursue dreams rather than passively waiting for them to be fulfilled: 'You stand in line, ya got lost in the jetstream'. It could be interpreted as an anthem to greed; it *was* the eighties, after all, and Van Halen's voracious appetite for more of everything – money, drugs, women – was in sync with that decade's

35

avaricious atmosphere. However, I prefer to think of it as a motivational, inspirational message – Van Halen, who have already succeeded beyond their wildest dreams, urging us to follow suit.

The instrumental finally diverges from three-chord simplicity, with tension-building ascending chords leading into a simple but catchy solo. After Dave's lecherous interlude, there's an extended out-chorus with Michael adding yobbish clout to the vocals and throwing in disco-ish octave bass runs. The song concludes with a return to the instrumental's rising chord pattern, now tweaked into 3/4 rather than 4/4 time – a sophisticated touch in this most primal of songs. As the final note fades, there's an almost-hidden payoff to Roth's earlier spoken section, as he tells the object of his attention, 'Look, I'll pay you for it, what the fuck!'. It's a masterpiece of cartoon caveman rock n' roll, which unsurprisingly became a firm fan favourite. As well as being a regular feature of Roth-era shows, the song has often been featured in televisual media, most notably in Richard Linklater's 2016 film, also titled 'Everybody Wants Some!', a college comedy set in 1980, which captures the spirit of the song to a tee.

'Fools' (Van Halen, Van Halen, Roth, Anthony)

'Fools' is one of several songs on the album dating back to 1974, first demoed with original bassist Mark Stone. A heavy blues shuffle, the song preaches youthful rebellion through a series of howling cliches, carried off with aplomb thanks to an effervescent performance. It opens with a relaxed bluesy exchange between guitar and vocals, Roth using the husky falsetto first unveiled on 'Light up the Sky'. After this spell of atmospheric noodling, Eddie cranks up the volume with a crashing chord and a burst of scattershot lead. The slippery, gnarly sound of the sludgy signature riff is produced by bending up to each note from a semitone below, while the steady, menacing rhythm is considerably weightier than the band's previous shuffles. Things are kept tight through the verse and bridge, before a release of pent-up energy on the chorus, with rattling round-the-kit drum fills, overdubbed bursts of lead, and those distinctive harmonies, making their first appearance on this album.

The original demo had verses of four lines each. Revising the song, Roth changed the words substantially, jettisoning many completely, and cutting the first two verses to two lines each and the third to an unconventional three. The lyrics are slapdash, co-opting well-worn tropes to convey a rejection of conformity and embrace of rock n' roll abandon. The first verse rebels against both 'school' and 'golden rules', an oft-used rhyme, dating back to Chuck Berry's 'School Days' (1957); the second rails against 'cleaning room' and 'pushing broom', a throwback to Roger Miller's 1965 country standard, 'King of the Road'. Roth delivers these sentiments with his customary panache, making them sound *almost* fresh. The third bridge contains the most authentic glimpse of Roth's philosophy: 'Don't need no class reunion, this circus just left town/ Why behave in public when you're living in a playground?'. He's left behind childhood conformity, joining the 'circus' of a travelling rock band, making the entire world his 'playground'. Eddie's solo is a blistering melange of searing blues and polyrhythmic flurries that threatens to fly off the handle. A new riff emerges for the last minute, over which Dave scats in a gravel-throated Louis Armstrong impersonation as the song fades – an indication of his esoteric frame of reference. 'Fools' may feel thrown-together, sloppy, and a tad over-long. However, it has a raw, reckless spontaneity that is the very essence of rock n' roll.

'Romeo Delight' (Van Halen, Van Halen, Roth, Anthony)

A take-no-prisoners rocker, 'Romeo Delight' is based on 'Get the Show on the Road', originally recorded for the 1977 demo. This serviceable up-tempo tune wasn't especially memorable but did feature a killer bridge, around which 'Romeo Delight' was created. Alex kicks off the song at a gallop as Eddie plays the riff in gritty, overdriven tapped harmonics. Mike's playing and tone are especially robust throughout, and his high fill introduces the riff proper – a proto-thrash metal assault, built around a chugging palm-muted low E, reminiscent of Black Sabbath's 'Symptom of the Universe' (1975). The verses start with a crashing chord, then dramatically fall quiet, with Alex and Mike maintaining a tense, ticking pulse, and Eddie adding sinuous, slurred, volume-swelled chords. The foreboding tone creates a perfect backdrop for Roth's film noir scenario. We've got all the classic ingredients, from the tough-talking protagonist, who can't tear himself away from his archetypal *femme fatale* ('a desperate woman, need a man with a gun') to the location ('high crime zone, city of lights'). It doesn't cohere into a complete narrative, but provides enough atmosphere and details for us to create our own picture – a visit to a party with the aforementioned 'desperate woman', a drunken altercation, a 'run-in with the law'. It's basically an account of a fairly typical evening for Dave, dramatised as a Chandleresque tale of LA's seedy underbelly. The chorus melds the bludgeoning main riff with the 'I'm taking whiskey to the party tonight' hook from 'Get the Show on the Road' over a new backing. A different chord sequence underpins Eddie's solo, Mike's bass keeping the sound full and propulsive beneath the high-octane shredding. The dynamics drop to a hushed, tense pulse as Dave murmurs 'ooh baby... feel my heartbeat' with heartbeat-like bass drum accents. As the tension peaks, the band explodes into a final chorus, with Dave adding manic whoops and screams on an extra vocal track. A drawn-out crash-ending concludes a track that combines savage intensity, catchy hooks and evocative lyrics, making it a sure-fire concert favourite throughout the Roth years.

'Tora! Tora!' (Van Halen, Van Halen, Roth, Anthony)

Not really a song, 'Tora! Tora!' is a brief instrumental introduction to 'Loss of Control'. Named after the Japanese code for the attack on Pearl Harbour, via the 1970 movie, *Tora! Tora! Tora!* (Fleischer/ Masuda/ Fukasaku), the track features two distinct sections. The first is an eerie soundscape, consisting of the reversed sound of Edward plucking his strings behind the nut, then depressing his vibrato bar until they fall slack onto the pickup. This reversed section ends with a taped sound effect – perhaps an approaching train, or gale-force wind. This fades to silence, then at 0.24, the second part begins with a ponderous, weighty riff, heavily indebted to Black Sabbath, complete with Iommi-ish guitar trills, and huge, elastic Bill Ward-esque drum fills. Roth adds to the ambience with air-raid siren wails and maniacal laughter, building a grim sense of foreboding for the eruption of energy that is to follow.

'Loss Of Control' (Van Halen, Van Halen, Roth, Anthony)
If 'Tora! Tora!' is a roller coaster crawling to its highest peak, 'Loss of Control' is a plummet to the bottom through rapid hairpin curves. Written after the Warner demo, before the debut album, the song reflects punk's velocity and nihilism. However, between Eddie's lightning-fingered boogie licks and Alex's pedal-to-the-metal swing, the effect is closer to turbo-charged rockabilly than generic 'punk'. The track has three sections: an ominous palm-muted low E rhythm; a full-pelt sequence of blistering rockabilly-meets-speed metal runs which underpins the song's only verse; and a different set of changes for Eddie's guitar solo – a coruscating blast of flanged riffs, culminating in a neat harmony with Mike's bass.

The track begins with the muted-E section, erupts into an instrumental 'verse', then returns to the E section, now with mock aircraft distress calls, ending in cries of 'mayday! mayday!'. The sole vocal verse features Mike harmonising with Dave's lively lead on alternating lines, and delivering a shrill cry of 'loss of control!' with amusing pearl-clutching hysteria. The lyrics (all four lines of them) find Roth embracing chaos, and complaining that he's 'wasting time, think I'd better go', because 'you're way too civilised'. Civilised behaviour was anathema to the band during these hotel-trashing, cocaine-fuelled days. They'd discover the consequences of this behaviour later, but in 1980, Van Halen seemed invincible, and 'Loss of Control' captures the glorious maelstrom of that time.

'Take Your Whiskey Home' (Van Halen, Van Halen, Roth, Anthony)
Another song dating back to the Mark Stone era, 'Take Your Whiskey Home' is a Led Zeppelin-influenced sultry mid-tempo blues rock strut. The 1974 demo reveals many elements already in place, with the riff, vocal line and most lyrics surviving largely unchanged in the final version. However, the original arrangement is a tad monotonous, rooted to the chord of G, with little dynamic variation. The LP version adds interest with a gritty, intimate acoustic intro, better-arranged backing vocals and a tension-building jump to the key of A for each chorus. Roth's protagonist bemoans the deterioration of his relationship due to his drinking, but if forced to make a choice between

living 'the good life' with her or continuing his wicked ways, admits, 'I like that bottle better than the rest'. Roth embodies the character, his gravelly moan by turns rueful and defiant, revelling in decadence, even as he despairs: 'it takes me at least halfway to the label/ before I can even make it through the night'. The song's dire portrayal of alcoholism probably seemed like rock n' roll fun in the fresh-faced days of 1974. However, with the benefit of hindsight, it seems like a dark foreshadowing of the demons that would haunt the Van Halen brothers in their later career.

Matching the sordid tone, Eddie's introductory riff has a languorous, drugged quality, each phrase ending in a lurching slide down the fretboard. The rhythm section chugs along with a steady restraint that makes the sudden dead stop at the end of each chorus startling. Eddie takes a four-bar solo before the third verse, full of slippery, unpredictable string bends, then unleashes a longer beak at 2:32. This starts out bluesy before bursting into wild flurries of tapping over the rhythm section's fiendishly complex offbeat accents. It's like a jazz-fusion take on Jimmy Page's stop-time solo from 'Whole Lotta Love' (1969). The song concludes by returning to the drawling introductory riff, with the sound of the tape being abruptly stopped on the final chord – a reminder of the physical nature of pre-digital recording. 'Take Your Whiskey Home' may not be an obvious stand-out, but its controlled power is a welcome contrast to the unhinged energy heard elsewhere, and the lyrics provide a glimpse of the growing darkness at the heart of the band's party lifestyle.

'Could This Be Magic?' (Van Halen, Van Halen, Roth, Anthony)
The album takes a stylistic left turn with 'Could This Be Magic?'. It's a charming, laid-back take on the ragtime-infused country blues of Mississippi John Hurt. Hurt cut a few obscure records in the late 1920s, then went back to farming, before a new generation discovered his music via Harry Smith's *Anthology of American Folk Music* (1952). His melodious approach and distinctive fingerpicking style influenced a generation of folk musicians. Dave is no John Hurt, but his guitar playing on 'Could This Be Magic?' is still a revelation, incorporating rhythmic boogie bass, delicately picked high notes and nifty melodic runs. Roth knew the Greenwich Village folk scene from an early age, spending time at his uncle Manny's club, the Café Wah?, where Bob Dylan and others played some of their earliest sets, and those roots are evident in this performance. Eddie plays acoustic slide guitar – a skill he learned especially for this recording. He weaves through the track, occasionally doubling the vocal melody, sometimes adding a lead flourish or tremulous chordal backing. A few fluffed notes add to the authentically spontaneous feel, and his tapping foot keeps the pulse in lieu of drums.

The lyric is a tongue-in-cheek wish-fulfilment fantasy that's also a metaphor for a lucky romantic encounter. Roth depicts a lonely islander pining for female company until his prayers are answered by a shipwreck.

By the second verse, the shipwrecked women are ashore, and Roth informs our protagonist with a wink that 'just could be, your boat is comin' in'. A harmonised refrain asks, 'Could this be magic, or could this be love?', marvelling at the mysteries of fate. With Dave's prompt of 'Edward... thank you', Eddie takes a brief solo, backed by Roth's solid rhythm. When the chorus returns, there's an extra high harmony, sung by country rocker and occasional Neil Young collaborator Nicolette Larson. Templeman produced her debut album in 1978, with Eddie guesting on 'Can't Get Away from you' (uncredited, as Roth was adamant that the band's brand shouldn't be diluted by outside projects). With this cameo, Larson returned the favour, becoming the first guest musician to appear on a Van Halen album. Although lightweight and whimsical, 'Could this be Magic?' is nevertheless a charming dip into an unexpected genre. It's also a perfect vehicle for cornball entertainer Roth, and shows Edward's remarkable adaptability as a musician, turning his hand to new styles and techniques at a moment's notice.

'In A Simple Rhyme' (Van Halen, Van Halen, Roth, Anthony)

To close the album, Van Halen selected another song first recorded in 1974. As befits an early composition, their formative influences are clearly on display, with obvious nods to The Who and Led Zeppelin, particularly the latter's 'The Song Remains the Same' (1973). A gentle acoustic intro gives way to hyperactive snare rudiments. Given the song's primary influences, it's an inevitable *tour de force* for the drummer, who does a terrific job of channelling both John Bonham's muscular jazziness and Keith Moon's explosive drama. Mike also edges into the spotlight, his bass louder in the mix as he unleashes some John Entwistle-like high-end fills. The song's breathless gallop is suddenly interrupted by the surprisingly pretty chorus with its chiming 12-string arpeggios and gleaming harmonies. The second chorus leads to a lush, mid-tempo interlude. Roth croons, 'you're gonna hear the angels singing' over appropriately angelic harmonies and Jimmy Page-like 12-string jangle, before a scream brings us back to blasting power chords and a sizzling guitar solo.

On earlier demos, Dave's vocal sounds awkward and constrained, as though unsure how to phrase the lyrics over the frenetic backing. Here, he sounds much more comfortable, with a half-sung, half-spoken delivery, bursting with personality. The lyrics are uncharacteristically wholesome and almost twee, reflecting the naivete of a young lyricist who hasn't yet found his voice: 'She made the mountains sing... she made an angel sigh' etc. The wit, wordplay and sense of character that are hallmarks of Roth's writing are absent, although his exuberance masks any textual deficiencies. The final chorus leads to a mellow coda, closing the album with soft arpeggios and soothing harmonies. Or so it appears, until, after a pause, a thumping tom fill introduces a few bars of grinding, discordant riffing, which fades as the record ends (on the CD, it comes to a dead stop). This instrumental, called 'Growth', was in development at the time of recording. There was a vague plan to begin the next record with it, creating a sense of continuity, but that never came to fruition, leaving 'Growth' as a curious punctuation mark to this ragged-but-glorious album.

Fair Warning (1981)

Personnel:
David Lee Roth: lead vocals
Edward Van Halen: guitar, backing vocals
Michael Anthony: bass, backing vocals
Alex Van Halen: drums
Recorded at Sunset Sound Recorders, Hollywood, March – April 1981
Produced by Ted Templeman
Engineered by Don Landee and Gene Meros
Record label: Warner Brothers
Release date: 29 April 1981
Highest chart position: US: 5, UK: 49
Running time: 31:11
Current edition: 2019 reissue

Van Halen entered 1981 on an upward trajectory, with no outward signs of anything amiss. Each of their albums had been more successful than the last and they played to adoring sell-out crowds wherever they went. They enjoyed all the perks of rock stardom, whether that meant joining the international party set like Dave, or marrying a bona fide Hollywood starlet, as Edward did, getting hitched to Valerie Bertinelli in April of that year. All they needed to do to ensure continued success was stick to the proven formula. However, Eddie wasn't content to rest on his laurels. Early on, he had welcomed Templeman's approach of recording the band as close to live as possible, but by 1981, the much more confident and experienced guitarist had developed a strong interest in studio craft. For the next LP, Templeman was again keen to work quickly, capturing a spontaneous, live sound. However, while the basic tracks were recorded in this familiar manner, Eddie grew close to engineer Donn Landee, remaining in the studio after hours with him to add layers of overdubs and experiment with synthesisers. This resulted in a denser, more complex-sounding record – a true studio creation rather than a mere representation of a live performance.

Much of Eddie's new music was noticeably darker and heavier, with little of Van Halen's trademark party ambience. This reflected the changing mood within the band, as the giddy first flush of success faded and relationships between members – especially Eddie and Dave – began to sour. Roth responded to these mean, brooding sounds with lyrics reflecting a bleaker outlook on life. The tongue-in-cheek wit was now tempered with a newfound cynicism. There was still fun to be had, but it was of the sordid, desperate kind, far removed from the wholesome SoCal sunshine. In part, Roth's change of attitude stemmed from a trip to Haiti, which gave him his first up-close encounter with poverty and deprivation. Unlike the Van Halen brothers, who grew up with considerable hardship, Roth had led a comfortable middle-class existence, and this brush with genuine third-world conditions shook him to his core. In his autobiography, he explains:

42

It was around this time – hang it on a hook called Haiti – that the world, to an *increasingly lesser* degree, revolved around myself ... My lyrics and my general tone began to alter subtly. I started writing titles like *Fair Warning* or 'Mean Streets'. Those were not celebration songs.

The album's packaging matched the dark material contained therein, featuring details from *The Maze* (1953), by Canadian artist William Kurelek. This disturbing allegorical work addressed the artist's struggles with mental health, presenting a series of scenes representing contributary factors in his mental illness as the contents of his split-open skull. The album sleeve focused on a few of these, including a small child being beaten by a bully while others watch and point; a man determinedly running headlong into a wall (Kurelek's representation of the futility of courage); and another bound to a conveyor belt, headed for death, as a clock attached to his feet counts away his life. It's a mesmerising painting, and fascinating album art, but unlikely to appeal to fans drawn to the band by the radio-friendly likes of 'Dance the Night Away'.

Released on 29 April 1981, the album sold well but not as quickly as previous efforts. It looked set to become their first album to fail to go platinum, and manager Noel Monk resorted to the age-old dodgy industry practice of payola to buy traction with radio stations. With this boost, the album achieved platinum status by November. However, its relatively sluggish performance caused concern; Eddie had pushed the band in a progressive direction which, though not disastrous, had been a moderate commercial backfire. Now the pressure was on from Roth, Templeman and the label to get back into safer commercial territory, leading to more tension. In *Runnin' with the Devil*, Monk's memoir of his time managing the band, his assessment of *Fair Warning* is damning, describing it as 'an unusual album, but certainly not a great album' which 'lacked a single hummable track'. However, while Monk's book undoubtedly contains much truth, it's written from a place of bitterness which taints his judgement. Contemporary critics were generally positive. Even the punk and post-punk fixated *NME* managed a cautious thumbs-up, with Cynthia Rose praising the band's musicianship, showmanship, and ability to 'architect actual and varied songs' – a trait unusual in heavy rock, according to Rose. Though slow to catch on with fans, the album eventually achieved legendary status among the faithful, coming in at number 2 in a 2015 *Rolling Stone* readers' poll to find fans' favourite album, just behind the eponymous debut.

'Mean Street' (Van Halen, Van Halen, Roth, Anthony)

This vision of urban desperation is set to one of the band's toughest riffs, originally part of an earlier song, 'Voodoo Queen', which appeared on the 1977 demo. As well as paring down the arrangement and stripping away a clunky chorus, 'Mean Street' wisely jettisons the corny exoticism of 'Voodoo Queen' for something much grittier. Eddie plays a dazzling unaccompanied intro – a hyperactive blend of aggressive bass notes, high double stops and piercing melody. It sounds as though three people are playing at once as he simultaneously taps harmonics and frets notes with his right hand, rhythmically mutes the strings with his left, and uses his right thumb to 'slap' his low E string like a funk bassist. From this furious outburst, he launches into the main riff, the rhythm section establishing a driving funk groove behind him, like a hard rock version of New Orleans legends, The Meters. Alex plays hi-hat sixteenths while hitting every alternate sixteenth on his kick drum, creating a more nimble, danceable feel than the standard hard rock 'boom-boom-thwack'.

The riff drops an octave for the verse, making room for Dave's attitude-dripping vocal. His lyrics set the scene: 'At night I watch this stinking street, past the crazies on my block'. Roth has depicted edgy, street-level scenes before, but normally his narrator stands apart: the cool outsider. Here, he places himself amongst the 'poor boys' he describes, sharing their frustration and their yearning for 'new kicks', however violent and dangerous they may be. This is not to suggest, however, that Roth has become a documentarian, dispensing social realism; though bleak, 'Mean Street' is still hugely entertaining. There's a healthy gallows humour to Roth's punning wordplay, delivering lines like 'You know this ain't no through street – the end is dead ahead' with menacing relish. The chorus riff (originally the verse of 'Voodoo Queen') is a rising sequence of ringing chords over a rumbling bass pedal note. The band add harmonies but fittingly stop short of the Beach Boys brightness heard elsewhere. At the end of the second chorus, a new line – 'They're dancing now, out on Mean Street' – leads into a stop time interlude, transplanted from the original arrangement of 'She's the Woman', an early track that would resurface years later. Here, Eddie's phase-shifted guitar is a brief ray of sunlight edging through the clouds – a moment of spontaneous joy in this oppressive landscape. This moment cannot last, however, and as the band roars back in, Eddie overdubs a savage, needling solo. After a final verse and chorus, the band drops to a whisper, as Dave's dramatic monologue details the violence spawned by this life of squalor. As he yells,'Wait a minute! Somebody said fair warning? Lord, strike that poor boy down!', Eddie's pick slide mimics a ricocheting bullet, and the band crashes back in, with a whammy bar lead lurching over the churning outro riff as the song fades. It's a powerful, imaginative opener, setting the LP's tone: tough and challenging but also exciting.

'Dirty Movies' (Van Halen, Van Halen, Roth, Anthony)

Our voyage into the seedier side of life continues with this sordid tale of a prom queen turned porn star. A reverb-laden tom fill introduces a tight mid-tempo groove, with lush, chorused bass harmonics and lightly strummed guitar chords. Another guitar crashes into the left channel, tapping a blizzard of random notes that sound like scrambled digital data, culminating in an echoing clang, produced by striking the vibrato springs. Simultaneously, the right channel features Eddie playing electric slide. Having difficulty hitting the high notes cleanly during recording, he took drastic action, sawing off the lower horn of this valuable 1962 SG junior's body to ease upper-fret access! After a tense chromatic ascent, the track hits full stride with a crunching, down-tuned riff and a woozy, lugubrious slide melody.

Rather than relating our main character's story episodically, Roth's lyrics introduce her as an image on-screen: 'Who's that babe with the fabulous shadow?'. The bridge builds intrigue, dropping hints at her small-town origins as the music intensifies. Finally, the second verse provides the character's back story in two bluntly-effective lines: 'Daddy's little cutie chasin' some damn rainbow/ Got the big deal in the back of a limo', Dave's knowing delivery ensuring that we don't miss his meaning. On paper, the chorus ('Pictures on a silver screen/ greatest thing you've ever seen/ Now her name is up in lights') describes the American dream – the small-town girl making it big. However, the vocals' mordant tone implies the grubby cynicism behind the supposed glamour. The second bridge leads to an upbeat instrumental, then back to the mellow bass harmonics. Roth-as-hometown-cinemagoer muses, 'Hey, you remember when that girl was prom queen?'. The rhythm section hits a hard funk groove, representing the raunchy on-screen action that prompts catcalls and wolf-whistles. A final bridge confirms that 'Now that they've seen it, now they believe it' – our protagonist's loss of innocence is complete. After one more chorus, Roth's cry of 'Lights! Camera! Aaaaction!' ends the song. The track's killer riffs and creative arrangement combine with Roth's witty storytelling to terrific effect. Also, it's unusual for a band not known for sexual prudishness to critique the grubby, exploitative side of the adult film industry, albeit with tongue firmly in cheek.

'Sinner's Swing!' (Van Halen, Van Halen, Roth, Anthony)

The album hits top gear with this frenetic, jive-talking shuffle, named after Max Fleischer's 1930 animated short, *Swing You Sinners!*. There's a bebop-like quality to the song's blistering tempo, off-kilter accents and rhythmic elasticity; the main riff could be a Dizzy Gillespie horn part, with its explosive stop-start rhythm, although there's nothing jazzy about the down-tuned growl of Eddie's guitar. Mike plays the start of each phrase, then sits out, allowing Alex's snare to propel the track. The bridge has a more solid rock groove, with the vocals trading call-and-response lines. The chorus hook of 'Get-get-get-get-get out and push!' is sung in three-part harmony, while the guitar adds a counter-melody between lines. A wild solo starts with a crazed vibrato bar whinny, followed by volatile tapped triplets, which almost career out of control, before snapping back on track for another chorus. The final verse drops to just vocal and guitar, this sudden intimacy adding menace to Roth's threat/promise 'Soon you'll see my silhouette a-darkening your door'. The final chorus extends into a fade-out, with Roth adding a final 'all you sinners, swing!' just before the music dies away.

The lyrics again evoke the tough-talking melodrama of pulp fiction. Roth's narrator sounds like a 1940s detective, fleeing a dreaded adversary: 'Danger in the rear-view mirror, there's trouble in the wind... the menace is loose again'. It emerges, however, that the 'menace' is a dangerously attractive woman, the song a dramatisation of an attempt to get laid! This theme continues in verse two, with the girl's indifference to our narrator's advances described as though she's an uncooperative witness in a criminal trial: 'You'd be sitting pretty, but you try to take the fifth/ Wearing out my welcome, guess I'd better save my breath'. In a genre filled with hackneyed songs about seduction and sex, this take is refreshingly inventive. Though not the LP's most celebrated track, 'Sinner's Swing' is the purest example of Van Halen's ebullient spontaneity on this brooding, complex record.

'Hear About It Later' (Van Halen, Van Halen, Roth, Anthony)

Closing side one, this defiant statement of consequence-free individualism features an arresting, inventive arrangement. It's introduced by warm, clean guitar, drenched in swirling flanger. The ringing arpeggios are atypical for heavy rock, stylistically closer to Andy Summers of The Police, who were peaking commercially in 1981. The opening motif – based around A and D chords, with ringing open strings creating yearning suspensions – becomes the song's main riff. After the verse takes us to a jangling D major, the bridge trickily switches time signature for a couple of bars before the main riff returns to underpin the chorus, now with added harmonies.

Meanwhile, Roth is on raucous form, bellowing, crooning, yelping, and occasionally sounding on the cusp of laughter. His defiant sneer matches the lyrics, which protest that he wants to be left to do as he pleases, without having to 'hear about it later' from demanding girlfriends, neighbours with the temerity to request peace and quiet, or anyone else. Unlike the romantic outsider of earlier lyrics, the loner-narrator of 'Hear About it Later' sounds browbeaten, pleading 'I've been tried and convicted, it's winner take all'. With tension growing within Van Halen, Roth's world-conquering idealism is becoming world-weary cynicism. After a gloriously melodic middle eight, we're plunged into a contrasting musical setting, stripping away layers of sound, leaving only minimal drums and bass. Eddie's adventurous solo blends more traditional bluesy motifs with polyrhythmic barrages of tapping, slashing fretboard slides and atonal alarm-klaxon sounds, magically leading back up to a reprise of the middle eight. The extended out-chorus gathers momentum, with the lead guitar building to a dive-bombing frenzy. Rumbling double kicks increase the intensity before the track concludes with a carefully-composed flourish. It's a testament to the band's skill as songwriters and arrangers that they can blur genre conventions and push boundaries while still sounding accessible. Dave's ability to graft catchy melodies and relatable, witty lyrics onto Edward's challenging music continued to bear fruit, even as their personal relationship grew more tenuous.

'Unchained' (Van Halen, Van Halen, Roth, Anthony)

In three and a half minutes, 'Unchained', encapsulates everything that made early Van Halen so special: an iconic riff, belting singalong chorus and blazing solo, married to lyrics which embody the band's philosophy while also sounding cool, and an infectious, poppy energy that offsets dizzying musical complexity. The main riff finds Eddie using drop-D tuning, maintaining a throbbing low pedal below shifting major and suspended 4th chords. This harmonic complexity has more in common with prog or jazz fusion than blues/pentatonic-based hard rock, although the energy and immediacy of the playing here are rarely heard in the cerebral prog and fusion genres. In the verse, Eddie's single note line weaves around the vocal with snarling pinch harmonics and deft melodic touches. The complexity increases in the bridge as the driving 4/4 pulse is disrupted by wild, choppy time changes, jumping unpredictably between bars of three and four beats. Roth's vocal line blithely coasts over this, creating a memorable hook from the confounding rhythmic maze.

The track slips back into gear for the chorus, sung over the main riff with big, anthemic harmonies. The vocal melody has a dark D minor tonality over the guitar part's D major voicing, creating an unusual but effective musical tension. Between the second and third choruses, Eddie takes a brief, beautifully structured solo over the tricky bridge, balancing divebombing harmonics and tapped flourishes with speech-like phrasing and graceful melodic touches. The band hushes after the third chorus while Dave ribs Ted Templeman about his fancy suit, with Roth's cry of 'Hey man, that suit is you!' cribbed from The Coasters' 1960 R&B novelty, 'Shoppin' for Clothes'. Templeman had dressed nicely for a meeting he was attending later, attracting Roth's satirical attention. This moment was recreated for tape, with Templeman interjecting a weary 'C'mon Dave, gimme a break' over the talkback, eliciting the response, 'one break, comin' up!' as the band bursts into a final chorus.

The lyrics describe the urge to escape mundanity's shackles to grasp your dreams, and the people from your old life who reappear once that success is realised. The concept is similar to that of 'Little Dreamer', albeit expressed in much more aggressive terms. The verses find a defiant Roth half-singing, half-yelling, 'I don't ask for permission, this is my chance to fly'. The bridge introduces a girl who has resurfaced now that our narrator has a 'fat city address', described with Chandlerian flair as 'blue-eyed murder in a size five dress'. The refrain of 'Unchained, yeah you hit the ground running' reflects the unstoppable momentum Van Halen had gathered in the short time since their Sunset strip days. Over the final chorus, Eddie's overdubbed lead builds from low, rhythmic octaves to soaring high melodic lines, before plunging to sub-sonic depths with a final divebomb. Although never a hit, 'Unchained' showcases the band at the zenith of their powers. A 2011 *Rolling Stone* readers' poll named it the fans' all-time favourite Van Halen song, and listening today, you really can't argue.

'Push Comes to Shove' (Van Halen, Van Halen, Roth, Anthony)

Built on a smoky R&B groove, 'Push Comes to Shove' was originally envisioned as a reggae track. The genre had recently started to infiltrate the US mainstream, and Roth – the band member most attuned to both black music and prevailing commercial trends – was keen to explore the style. In the end, although Eddie's offbeat rhythm guitar accents hint at a reggae feel, Mike's upfront disco-infused bassline and Alex's restrained-but-propulsive groove push the track towards funk territory, with Eddie's lead adding a sprinkling of jazz. The rhythm section introduces the track, Mike playing a slinky octave bassline as Eddie's guitar gently insinuates itself with sinuous volume swells. A spoken vignette sets the scene; a cold dressing room, our narrator trying to stave off the boredom and loneliness of the inevitable post-show comedown. Roth's lyrics are unusually reflective, ruefully depicting the difficulty of sustaining meaningful relationships while living the supposedly glamorous life of a touring musician. 'Some people live apart, they break your heart so damn easy', he moans, husky with world-weary resignation. The second verse is especially telling, with our narrator acknowledging that, while the life he leads looks idyllic from the outside, he feels like a 'stranger here in paradise', complaining that 'it feels like 40 days and 40 nights since someone used my first name, including you'. For all the fleeting encounters on offer, his hunger for real human closeness feels like a biblical famine. It's an unexpected insight from Dave, who generally embodies the rock star fantasy in all its shallow glory. However, it's refreshing to glimpse relatable fragility behind the outrageous facade

The bluesy minor-key groove reinforces the brooding tone, with Eddie's guitar alternating between choppy high chords and muted bass-string runs. The bridge introduces a heavily-chorused clean guitar, playing a sparkling counter-melody before the chorus falls back to the core instrumentation. For the solo, the rhythm shifts to a less propulsive, more syncopated Latin-American feel. Eddie's lead soars adventurously, with keening harmonic-minor melodies and palm-muted sweep-picking (rapid arpeggios played with a single sweeping motion of the pick). Although reluctant to discuss his influences beyond the formative inspirations of Cream-era Clapton and Tony Iommi, Eddie had recently enthused about English prog/fusion virtuoso Alan Holdsworth, who he heard playing in Bill Bruford's eponymous band. Holdsworth's influence is evident here, adding yet another dimension to Eddie's playing. He complained that Templeman made him record multiple takes of this solo, but the finished product is worth the effort. There's a key change to B minor for the outro, the band letting off steam as the track fades. It's a low-key number but a fine piece of work, with real subtlety and depth.

'So This Is Love?' (Van Halen, Van Halen, Roth, Anthony)

On an otherwise dark LP, 'So This is Love?' is a lone beacon of positivity, at least at face value. It's an upbeat number about a man who has found the girl of his dreams and wants to tell the world. The lyrics are packed with wonderfully hyperbolic descriptions of this newfound sensation, such as 'man needs love to live, I'm the living proof/ Catch that smile and I hit the roof'. The chorus asks, 'So this is love?', our incredulous narrator is unable to believe it's really happening to him. How charming and innocent! Some fans, however, are convinced that, in keeping with the album's cynical tone, the girl, 'on the corner... lookin' so fine' is a sex worker, which would cast the song in a more sardonic light. The original title and first line of the chorus was 'Flesh and Blood', which makes the physical nature of the 'love' in question clearer. The track also originally carried the subtitle '(Banana Oil)', a reference which thankfully didn't survive the final cut.

Nevertheless, potentially unseemly undertones aside, it's still possible to enjoy 'So This is Love?' as a simple, upbeat love song, and the music matches this interpretation perfectly. It begins with an ebullient rhythm section playing a tight, bouncy shuffle – a muscular take on classic soul shuffles like Martha and the Vandellas' 'Heatwave' (1963) or Jackie Wilson's 'I Get the Sweetest Feeling' (1968). Roth sings the verses with appropriately soulful gusto, handling the wordy lyrics with wonderfully elastic phrasing. Eddie plays a quiet chordal vamp until a rattling snare fill introduces the blasting bridge. The bright harmonies of the chorus hook betray no cynicism, whatever the lyrics' underlying intent. The band even add handclaps to the second chorus, bolstering the wholesome sixties pop-soul feel. The soul vibe carries into Eddie's solo, which utilises saxophone like phrasing reminiscent of the great King Curtis in its opening four bars. The solo is pieced together from four different recordings, a task Landee handed over to Eddie himself – signalling the guitarist's increasingly hands-on interest in the recording process. A stop-time chorus leads to an ecstatic out-chorus, with Roth whooping up a storm while Eddie adds a hypnotic high D drone, before winding up with some flashy heroics. Released in June 1981, the single disappointingly peaked at 110 on the *Billboard* chart. Perhaps the disturbing picture sleeve (a detail of the bullying scene from *The Maze*) didn't help, but it's still a travesty that this terrific pop song wasn't hugely successful. Still, it remains popular with fans, and reappeared in the band's 2007 reunion tour sets, with the bass intro affording Wolfgang Van Halen a moment in the spotlight.

'Sunday Afternoon in The Park' (Van Halen, Van Halen, Roth, Anthony)

'Sunday Afternoon in the Park' is a menacing instrumental synth/drums duet, representing Eddie's first recorded use of synthesizers after playing electric piano on the previous LP. Here, he plays an Electro-Harmonix Mini-Synthesizer (a small keyboard synth, not to be confused with the same company's Micro-Synth, designed for use with a guitar or bass) through his flanger pedal. The track creeps along ominously in C minor, Eddie manipulating the synth's filters and kicking the flanger on and off to make guttural electronic snarls over the drums' monolithic thunder. A somewhat more melodic section in 7/8 begins at 0:35, moving briefly to a brighter major key before plunging back to the original punishing pattern, Eddie's synth gurgling nastily like a wounded creature retreating to its lair. The track recedes to a low growl, as the contrastingly frantic synth of the following track cross-fades in.

The cosy title is savagely ironic. In Valerie Bertinelli's memoir, *Losing It – and Gaining My Life Back, One Pound at a Time* (2008), she claims, 'Ed told me that I'd inspired the song 'Sunday Afternoon in the Park', a heavy, grinding instrumental. He said it was us fighting all the time'. It's an oddity for Van Halen, its harsh, brutal minimalism sounding closer to the proto-industrial style of Throbbing Gristle or Cabaret Voltaire than good-time rock. The track unexpectedly resurfaced in the 1990s when Michael featured it as part of his bass solo in live shows, using the aforementioned Micro-Synth to replicate Eddie's keyboard sound.

'One Foot Out the Door' (Van Halen, Van Halen, Roth, Anthony)

The album closes with this terse blast of hectic synth rock. Consisting of just a single verse and chorus with minimal instrumentation, it continues the preceding track's stark feel, perhaps reflecting its hasty creation and late addition to the album, when the band practically had 'one foot out the door' of the studio. Some commentators, including *Eruption* authors Brad Tolinski and Chris Gill, consider these final two tracks to be 'incomplete sketches'. Though not totally unjustified, this view does a disservice to forward-looking pieces of music which, if not fully realised, show the band's restless creativity, and anticipate the increasing role technology would play in rock music over the following decade.

The song begins with a rumbling synth line. After a tom-tom build-up, Alex kicks straight into the verse at a gallop. Despite the track's futuristic trappings and off-kilter harmonic progressions, Dave still turns it into a blues song, albeit an austere, furious one. Roth's frustrated narrator has been denied a weekend of illicit passion by the sudden return of his lover's terrifying husband, prompting a hasty exit: 'I got one foot out the door, tryin' to hit the road/ Ain't no match for your mean old man, I think it's time to roll'. This is firmly in the blues tradition, recalling 'One Way Out', recorded by Chicago legend Elmore James, and released posthumously in 1965, which finds its narrator imploring his lover to 'raise your window baby, I ain't going out that door/ There's a man downstairs, he may be your husband, I don't know'. As the 'chorus' ends with Roth speeding into the distance, pledging 'no coming back, back for more', Eddie delivers a startlingly aggressive solo. He channels his frustration and anger through the guitar, rattling out furious bursts of notes and shaking the vibrato bar as though trying to choke the life out of the instrument. Finally, he latches onto a catchy double-stop riff just as the track fades. It's an unusual but exhilarating end to the album, its blend of aggression and dark humour fitting the spirit of this troubled, thrilling LP perfectly.

Diver Down (1982)

Personnel:
David Lee Roth: lead vocals, synthesiser on 'Intruder', acoustic guitar and harmonica on 'The Full Bug'
Edward Van Halen: guitar, backing vocals, synthesiser on 'Dancing In The Street'
Michael Anthony: bass, backing vocals
Alex Van Halen: drums
Additional personnel:
Jan Van Halen: clarinet on 'Big Bad Bill'
Recorded at Sunset Sound Recorders & Amigo Studios, January – March, 1982
Produced by Ted Templeman
Engineered by Donn Landee
Record label: Warner Brothers
Release date: 14 April 1982
Highest chart position: US: 3, UK: 36
Running time: 31:04
Current edition: 2019 reissue

Shaken by the relatively poor commercial performance of *Fair Warning,* there was a feeling in the Van Halen camp that change was needed. Eddie particularly felt that the non-stop cycle of touring and recording was preventing them from developing musically. They would go straight from tour to studio, expected to hammer out a platinum album within two to three weeks. There was rarely a break for an extended writing period, so the band had to scrape together material on the road or ransack their stockpile of pre-Warner deal originals and repertoire of covers to fill an LP. Manager Noel Monk agreed that a change of pace was needed, explaining in *Runnin' With The Devil* that the plan was to 'rest and recharge our batteries, and take the time to write and record a masterpiece'. Roth, however, was reluctant to allow the band to slip from public consciousness, fearing their fickle audience might move on if Van Halen were away for a full year. As a compromise, he suggested a standalone single – a first for the band. The idea was to cover a popular favourite, keeping the band in the public eye and hopefully putting them back in the charts, without the pressure of an attendant album or tour. Roth suggested Martha and the Vandellas' 1964 smash, 'Dancing in the Street', but Eddie couldn't figure out how to make it sound like Van Halen, so the band settled on Roy Orbison's 1964 hit, '(Oh) Pretty Woman'. Aided by a suitably ridiculous music video, which made a splash on the new-fangled music channel, MTV (before being banned), the single was the band's most successful yet. Unfortunately, it also prompted significant pressure from Warner Brothers to follow up quickly with an album – exactly what the band had been hoping to avoid.

Having not expected to record again so soon, they had little new material, so relied more heavily than ever on covers. This particularly suited

Templeman, who knew the band's capacity for turning dusty standards into sure-fire contemporary hits, and Roth, who was able to exercise his more 'showbiz' inclinations – a foretaste of things to come in his solo career. With Eddie having little interest in playing other people's songs and feeling disengaged from the project, there were no late-night overdubbing sessions with Landee this time. Instead, the band returned to the almost-live approach favoured by Templeman, delivering the album in a mere 12 days on a budget of $46,000 – less than their debut had cost. The simple, striking cover art is the 'diver down' flag, used to indicate that a scuba diver is submerged. Roth was fond of claiming that the cover and title were a metaphor for the hidden depths lying beneath the surface of the band. Monk, contrastingly, claimed the title was actually a crude pun about cunnilingus: 'dive 'er down'. Either or both may be true, but I prefer Roth's story to Monk's, who, by the time he wrote his book in 2017, was bitterly invested in making the band members seem like juvenile imbeciles.

The album was a great success, selling faster than its predecessor, and hitting number three on the *Billboard* chart – their highest placing to date. Critics weren't as kind to it as the fans, with *Rolling Stone*'s review claiming that the band were 'running out of ideas'. The members of the band don't tend to look back on the record fondly either, with Eddie practically disowning it in later years. However, it's a hugely enjoyable lucky dip of a record. Granted, it feels more like a superior 'leftovers and rarities' collection than a coherent studio album, but everything on there is terrific; the covers are transformed by Van Halen's unique magic; the originals show the band's terrific range – from the delicate 'Secrets' to the boisterous 'The Full Bug'; and, despite his lack of interest in the LP, Eddie's playing shines, with the variety of the material showcasing his all-round virtuosity like never before.

'Where Have All the Good Times Gone?' (Ray Davies)

Following the success of 'You Really Got Me', it made sense for the band to record another of the Kinks songs from their early repertoire. However, while the raw energy of that song matched Van Halen's style, 'Where Have All the Good Times Gone?' is a different beast. The Kinks' original is relatively laid-back, its attack softened by Ray Davies' lazily strummed acoustic and drawled vocals. This approach fits the despondent lyrics, which satirically long for a mythical lost age of innocence, but Van Halen weren't about to begin an LP with such lugubrious fare. Instead, they toss out the original arrangement, writing their own introduction and instrumental middle eight and cheekily co-opting Mick Ronson's growling hard rock riff from David Bowie's 1973 version of the song. Given the growing discord within the band, the world-weary lyrics are apt. However, Dave's delivery is anything but listless; if on The Kinks' recording, Davies sounds despairing at the loss of the bygone 'good times', Roth can't contain his irrepressible exuberance. With no overdubs, Eddie's guitar covers all bases, transitioning from chugging riffs to chiming arpeggios, melodic octave runs to snarling fills. The instrumental consists of belting syncopated power chords played over a bass pedal note, and decorated with slashing pick slides, vibrato bar warbling and Iommi-esque trills. There's not much more to the arrangement than that, nor does there need to be. The customary ultra-poppy harmonies appear on the chorus, and Eddie takes the riff up an octave going into the fade out, concluding this simple, effective reimagining of a pop classic.

'Hang 'Em High' (Van Halen, Van Halen, Roth, Anthony)

This explosive rocker began as 'Last Night', recorded for the 1977 demo. That track had an almost identical backing to 'Hang 'Em High', but with wordier, less-evocative lyrics and an awkward-sounding melody, which probably explains why it remained in the vault. When the song was hastily resurrected for *Diver Down,* Roth overhauled his contribution, keeping only the middle eight melody. The verse melody was replaced by a tuneless but effective double-tracked attitudinal drawl and the chorus was also totally re-written. The lyrics, formerly a hackneyed tale of a cheating girlfriend, were replaced by a striking montage of spaghetti western imagery featuring a character reminiscent of Clint Eastwood's 'Stranger'. Roth's fluency in the language of pulp fiction is a great asset, showcasing his economical storytelling and fondness for the 'lone outlaw' archetype. The enigmatic anti-hero, recognisable from countless horse-operas, is introduced with the phrase: 'Somewhere he lost his turn, now trouble seems to fit him like a glove'. The chorus fills in more details, depicting a fleeing outlaw who, if caught, is 'headed for the moon, they'll hang him high'. You can hear the galloping hooves of his pursuers in the relentless speed-metal-with-extra-swing assault of the rhythm section and Eddie's blistering proto-thrash riff. Although simple in terms of notes used, this is a dazzling display of surgically-precise right-hand technique, with rapid-fire palm-muting, meticulously-placed accents and harmonic squeals. Again, with no overdubs, the razor-sharp riffs, lead flourishes, ringing arpeggios and intricately composed solo are all played in a single breathtaking performance. The last chorus slows inexorably, suggesting the outlaw's pursuers have finally caught up with him. With a tremolo-picked ascending lead and double-kick flurry, the song crashes to a halt. 'Hang 'Em High' is a mysterious, exhilarating record showcasing an astounding group performance and was one of several deep cuts that returned to Van Halen's live sets during the reunion tours with Dave.

'Cathedral' (Van Halen, Van Halen, Roth, Anthony)

The first of two solo guitar showcases on this album, 'Cathedral', was a piece that Eddie had started to incorporate in his live solo spot during the 1981 tour. Less obviously spectacular than 'Eruption', it's possibly even more inventive – a staggering combination of virtuoso technique and imaginative use of effects to create a sound that many might struggle to identify as originating from a guitar. As Gene Santoro explains in *The Guitar: The History, The Music, The Players:*

> He's running a '61 Strat through a preset echo and chorus, simultaneously cutting the volume in and out, and hammering on a series of notes at the speed of the echo; the effect, as he intended, is a weird evocation of a church organ.

While the guitar's vintage is questionable (other sources cite a late-'50s model), this description illustrates the inspired alchemy employed by Eddie to bring to life the sounds he heard in his head, using an electric guitar to transport the listener to a cavernous, echoing sonic cathedral.

'Secrets' (Van Halen, Van Halen, Roth, Anthony)

With its delicate, airy sound, 'Secrets' represents quite a departure for the band. A burst of summery sunshine pop, tinged with autumnal melancholy, the song's sparkling 12-string jangle and crooned vocals are worlds away from the heavy rock listeners might expect. However, closer inspection reveals many familiar Van Halen traits still in evidence; the main riff is a series of shifting chords played over an unchanging pedal note, like 'Runnin' With the Devil' or 'Unchained'. The trademark harmonies are prominent and, amid the Byrds-like clean 12-string riffs (played on a Gibson EDS-1275 double-neck), Eddie still manages to sneak in an overdriven solo, tastefully blending moderate fireworks with beautifully structured lyrical passages.

The lyrics are a coming-of-age tale, depicting a free-spirited young woman venturing into the wide world, her steps 'making tracks in the winter snow'. She has no idea where she's going, except that 'she be headed where the thunder rolls', moving symbolically from purity and innocence to noise and danger. If the imagery seems un-Roth-like, it's because, as he told *Sounds*: 'The nucleus of the lyrics come from greeting cards and get-well cards that I bought in Albuquerque, New Mexico on the last tour, and they were written in the style of American Indian Poetry. 'May your moccasins leave happy tracks in the summer snows'.' Despite this mundane source of inspiration, Roth fashions a pleasingly enigmatic narrative to match Eddie's shimmering chords, delivering it with impressive sensitivity. Mike and Alex play a nimble shuffle, driving the song along with a lightness of touch that's surprising from such a powerhouse duo, and the overall effect is pleasantly disarming.

'Intruder' (Van Halen, Van Halen, Roth, Anthony)

Although listed as a standalone track, this brief, foreboding instrumental was conceived specifically as an introduction to '(Oh) Pretty Woman', after the band created a promo video that was nearly two minutes longer than the song! The sinister tone reflects the plot of the video, in which a nefarious hunchback and his two dwarf goons kidnap a beautiful woman, played by transsexual actor International Chrysis, before our heroes, dressed, improbably, as a samurai, a cowboy, Tarzan and Napoleon – come to the rescue. The track is built on a stomping drumbeat and a moody synth line, played by Dave, again proving his musical versatility, using the same Electro-Harmonix synth featured on *Fair Warning*. Over this, Eddie's guitar evokes alarm klaxons, blood-curdling screams, rattling chains and animal sounds, using nothing more than carefully manipulated feedback, creative vibrato bar abuse, and attacking the strings with a can of Schlitz malt liquor, a drink that the band consumed by the caseload. The track builds in intensity until, without breaking tempo, it segues into '(Oh) Pretty Woman'.

'(Oh) Pretty Woman' (Dees, Orbison)

Bursting from the churning darkness of 'Intruder', the opening chords of '(Oh) Pretty Woman' sound especially bright. The band's arrangement is no massive departure from Roy Orbison's original recording, keeping the bones of the song intact and fleshing them out with recognisable Van Halen characteristics – Eddie's divebombs and harmonics, Roth's cocksure showmanship, and Mike's brilliant harmonies. However, there are a couple of edits to the song, which appear to have been unintentional. During the rushed recording, the last two lines of the middle eight were compressed into a single "Cos I need you, need you tonight', and the line 'Is she walking back to me?' vanished from the outro. Luckily, neither omission significantly affects the integrity of the song, and they might be taken for deliberate edits if we didn't know otherwise.

This is the first Van Halen recording on which the main guitar is not panned hard left. Instead, guitars, vocals and bass all sit in the centre, with only the stereo spread of Alex's kit keeping the track from being completely mono. This initially-standalone single was targeted towards heavy MTV and radio rotation, so was mixed specifically to sound as punchy as possible through a mono television or portable radio. Eddie uses chorus on his guitar, adding a glossy sheen to his sound. He steers clear of power chords – that heavy metal staple – throughout, relying instead on big, open arpeggios, using poignant-sounding suspended 9th chords. The overall effect, though still boisterously exuberant, has more in common with the commercial pop/rock of The Police than the histrionics of the Sunset Strip rockers (Motley Crue, Ratt, *et al*) emerging in Van Halen's wake. This is a rare Van Halen recording with no guitar solo, a fact that undoubtedly irked Eddie, especially when it went on to become such a big hit. Nevertheless, for all Eddie's misgivings about the record's calculated commerciality, it's a great version of the song, bursting with energy and charm.

'Dancing In the Street' (Gaye, Hunter, Stevenson)

Roth's suggestion of this oft-covered 1964 Martha and the Vandellas classic for the supposed one-off single was rejected by Eddie. However, with an album's worth of material required at short notice, the idea resurfaced, and Roth decided to superimpose the song's melody over a distinctive synth riff Eddie had composed. This caused some friction, as Eddie justifiably felt that his original music had been co-opted to provide a hook for a cover, for which he'd receive no writing credit or publishing royalties. Nevertheless, the combination works brilliantly, breathing new life into a well-worn oldie, and creating a futuristic dance-rock hybrid – fresh-sounding but still packed with familiar trademarks.

The track begins with the synth that underpins the whole song, played on a Mini-Moog processed through a pitch shifter and Echoplex for a bubbling, ping-ponging effect. The band plays a repetitive, danceable groove, Eddie unusually utilising two rhythm guitar tracks throughout. The left channel doubles the synth line, adding occasional harmonic squeals, while a second part, mixed centrally, locks in with Mike's bass, playing simple power chords. The effect is a blend of the hypnotic electro-pop pioneered by Italian producer Giorgio Moroder and the band's more organic rock n' roll. As John Scanlan explains in *Van Halen: Exuberant California Zen Rock N' Roll*: 'It is as if someone had plugged Donna Summer's 'I Feel Love' into Eddie's ears as he slept, and this was what he remembered on waking'. Certainly, while retaining the melody and backing vocal hooks of the Vandellas' original, the accompaniment to Van Halen's version is closer in feel to Summer's 1977 disco smash than the Motown sound. Tempo-wise, it's slower than either – a funky mid-tempo strut that's dancefloor-friendly but with hard-rock weight. With Dave selling the song enthusiastically, Mike and Eddie providing their best girl-group harmonies and a searing guitar solo to boot, it's a belting slice of commercial pop-rock. Despite Eddie's distaste, it was a rightful success, providing the album's second US top 40 single and setting a precedent for further integration of synths into Van Halen's sound.

'Little Guitars (Intro)' (Van Halen, Van Halen, Roth, Anthony)
Eddie's second solo showcase on the record finds him playing nylon-strung acoustic for the first time since 'Spanish Fly'. Inspired by flamenco guitarist Carlos Montoya, the track highlights Eddie's remarkable resourcefulness as he recreates the sounds of flamenco with a technique that is all his own. As he explains in *Eruption*:

> I saw him on television, and he was doing these crazy things with his fingers. I knew it would take me years to learn how to fingerpick like him, so I came up with my own way to replicate what I liked about the sound of it.

It was relatively straightforward to simulate Montoya's *rasgueado* (a prolonged, percussive strum using the nails of each finger in quick succession) with a pick. However, Eddie was particularly taken with

Montoya's ability to pluck a melody on the bass strings with his thumb while simultaneously maintaining a tremolo-picked drone on his upper strings using his other fingers. Primarily a plectrum player, Eddie lacked the right-hand dexterity for this technique. However, he was able to create a Montoya-like bass run entirely with powerful left-hand hammer-ons and pull-offs, leaving his right hand free to tremolo-pick the upper strings. The effect is remarkable, sounding (to the untrained ear) as though he has studied flamenco for years. Although only 42 seconds long, the track is a perfectly formed composition and an evocative introduction to the full-length song that follows.

'Little Guitars' (Van Halen, Van Halen, Roth, Anthony)

The flamenco mood gives way to a loping drum groove, soon joined by a languid guitar riff over a heartbeat-like bass pedal. The track builds in intensity with off-beat chordal work, before kicking into double time for the verse. The main guitar track is played on a miniature copy of a Gibson Les Paul, made by luthier, Dave Petschulat, which is tuned three semitones above standard pitch due to its short scale length. The song was inspired by this instrument's unique tonal qualities, hence its tendency towards incisive, choppy high chordal work, rather than weighty riffs. Indeed, although the rhythm section packs its usual punch, there are few heavy rock hallmarks in the guitar part, its chorus-drenched, harmonically rich rhythm work evoking the pop-prog of later Genesis.

The lyrics are a charming, guileless ode to a certain 'senorita', with Roth displaying surprising sensitivity and reining in the machismo and innuendo. He can see she is concealing secret pain ('You say you're lonesome, just getting by, but you turn your eyes from me') and is eager to offer comfort ('Senorita, do you need a friend? I'm in love with you'). This simple, sweet sentiment is matched by one of the band's brightest pop melodies. Dave skilfully turns a rhythmically thorny fusion-inspired passage in which the regular 4/4 pulse is interrupted by a single bar of 3/4 into the song's main hook, with his irresistible 'Catch as catch, catch as catch can' refrain. He even manages to reference the diminutive instrument on which the song was composed: 'When I see you, all your little guitars sing to me'. This leads to an instrumental featuring a swooning slide guitar over a backdrop of delicate arpeggios. After a final verse, an extra guitar adds some rock swagger before the band drops out, leaving the mini guitar's staccato chords to end the track alone. 'Little Guitars' was never a single, but sounds like a hit; a tremendous slice of progressive guitar pop, which finds Dave and Eddie's artistic partnership flourishing, despite personal differences.

'Big Bad Bill (Is Sweet William Now)' (Ager, Yellen)

The band reached waaay back for this old chestnut, written in 1924 by the team behind standards like 'Happy Days are Here Again' and 'Ain't she Sweet?'. A hit for both Billy Murray and Margaret Young that year, it was recorded by a wide range of artists over the decades that followed, including pop-jazz vocalist Peggy Lee (1962) and country legend Merle Haggard (1973). This track is the only recording of the Van Halen brothers playing alongside their father, Jan, who, at Roth's suggestion, added clarinet. Jan, a respected jazz musician in the Netherlands, had been unable to support the family solely through music in the US. More recently, he had fallen out of practice, having lost a finger in an industrial accident, which understandably severely hampered his playing. Nevertheless, with much encouragement (and beer!), he turned in a lovely performance, his mellifluous tone and gentle vibrato recalling Benny Goodman – just what the track's 1930s small-group swing arrangement needed. Eddie plays an authentic-sounding swing rhythm, comping like Eddie Condon on an arch-top Gibson acoustic. Alex keeps time on hi-hat, adding gentle brushed snare, while Michael achieves a passably double bass-like effect using a guitarron, the six-stringed acoustic bass guitar usually found in Mariachi bands.

The song tells the tale of Bill, a notorious Louisville hoodlum transformed by married life into an easy-going, domesticated doormat. It's a gift to born-Vaudevillian Roth, whose relaxed phrasing and hep-cat interjections ('I *likes* that!') recall Cab Calloway and Louis Armstrong. The final chorus is extended, with an off-mic Roth voicing Bill's wife's commands to 'do the dishes' and 'mop up that floor!', before a suitably cornball ending. It's not something most rock bands would consider recording, and probably left some fans nonplussed. However, it's great, silly fun, and there's a sweet poignancy in hearing the two generations of Van Halens playing together, with Jan finally having a moment in the spotlight after years of toil, disappointments and indignities.

'The Full Bug' (Van Halen, Van Halen, Roth, Anthony)
After that stylistic detour, 'The Full Bug' takes us back to Van Halen's roots. It's a hyperactive power-blues shuffle with a killer guitar riff, drums that sound like a herd of charging rhinos, and innuendo-laden lyrics. The track begins gently, with Roth accompanying himself on acoustic guitar, affecting a Howlin' Wolf-like growl. The close-miked intimacy is interrupted by an obnoxious divebomb, and then we're whisked off at a brisk pace, with Billy Cobham-style double kicks, and a great, spiky riff built on a series of squealing pinch harmonics. Alex notches up the intensity in the chorus, switching his already busy kick pattern to a stream of thundering triplets as Eddie plays a Chuck Berry rock n' roll rhythm and vocal harmonies add pop polish. Eddie's solo commences in the same Chuck Berry vein, with a tremolo-picked double-stop run, but rapidly diverges. A swiftly picked passage, including some off-kilter note choices, culminates in a jazzy motif played by the band in unison. Dave takes over with a very accomplished harmonica solo, again giving lie to the persistent myth that he was a mere showman, rather than a 'real musician'. After a reprise of the guitar/vocal

intro, one more chorus leads us to a fade-out, with Roth's much-abused voice audibly cracking as he ad-libs wildly.

The lyrics are addressed from an impoverished suitor to his materialistic 'precious sweetheart', explaining that the luxurious lifestyle she's seen in the media pales by comparison with the love he offers. Unsurprisingly, this wholesomeness is undercut with punning double-entendres. Take, for instance, the final couplet of the chorus: 'Takers need a giver, this much you understand/ All I wanna give you, woman, is the best part of a man'. Of course, this could refer to his heart, but could equally mean an entirely different organ, giving the song a considerably less sentimental slant! All in all, 'The Full Bug' proves that, even as they branched out, Van Halen still had their knack for over-the-top, bawdy rock n' roll. The song was among the numerous fan favourites revived for Roth's return, regularly appearing in 2012 tour setlists.

'Happy Trails' (Evans)

This song was written by Dale Evans, and originally recorded by Evans and her husband, Roy Rogers, as the closing theme for his popular western TV series, *The Roy Rogers Show* (1951-1957). It was one of several novelty songs that Van Halen could sing in a capella four-part harmony, and an impromptu version featured on their 1977 demo. The version that closes *Diver Down* is basically the same arrangement, slightly tightened-up, but still with some amusingly wobbly moments, the band members sounding rather less than sober. After making a show of finding his note, Dave leads off with a 'bom-ba-dee-da' bassline. Eddie, Mike and Alex (making a rare vocal appearance) add their corny harmonies, sounding like an enthusiastic if under-rehearsed barbershop quartet. They switch to background 'aaahhs' during the bridge, as Roth takes the lead, hamming it up beautifully and lapsing into an Al Jolson impersonation on the line 'Just sing a song and think 'bout sunny weather'. Roth adds an ambitious flourish to his bass part on the final line, and the band sustain the last chord until they collapse into giggles at the silliness of it all. It's a fun way to send the audience home at the end of this highly entertaining rag-tag variety show of an album, and the band frequently closed their live sets the same way during the remainder of Roth's tenure.

1984 (1984)

Personnel:
David Lee Roth: lead vocals
Edward Van Halen: guitar, keyboards, backing vocals
Michael Anthony: bass, synth bass on 'I'll Wait', backing vocals
Alex Van Halen: drums
Recorded at 5150 Studios, June – October 1983
Produced by Ted Templeman
Engineered by Don Landee
Record label: Warner Brothers
Release date: 9 January 1984
Highest chart position: US: 2, UK: 15
Running time: 33:22
Current edition: 2019 reissue

Diver Down had been a significant commercial success for Van Halen, but its rushed production, the control exerted by Roth and Templeman, and the number of covers included had infuriated Eddie. He was determined to take back control for the follow-up. The first step was to build a home studio, forcing Templeman and the band to meet him on his own turf, and allowing him to choose his own recording schedule. The idea of building his own studio was planted in the Spring of 1982 when Eddie went to visit avant-rock maverick Frank Zappa. The famously curmudgeonly Zappa had been unusually complimentary about Eddie's playing, and his 12-year-old son, Dweezil, was a huge fan. Eddie jammed with Zappa and his then-'stunt guitarist', Steve Vai, who later played in Roth's solo band. The session took place in the 'Utility Muffin Research Kitchen', Zappa's studio, and Eddie was struck by the creative freedom and convenience that it offered. Eddie agreed that he and Donn Landee would produce a single ('My Mother is a Space Cadet' (1982)) for Dweezil and his band. This gave him some hands-on production experience, and further solidified his partnership with Landee, crucial in his attempt to wrest control of the band's direction from Templeman and Roth. Landee was also enlisted to oversee the creation of 5150 studios (named after the police code for an escaped mental patient) on Eddie's Coldwater Canyon property while the band were out on tour.

Eddie's insistence on a change in recording practices wasn't the only cause of tension in the run-up to *1984*. While Dave spent his post-*Diver Down* tour break adventuring in the Amazon, Edward lent his skills to other musical projects, scoring for film and TV, collaborating with Queen's Brian May on the *Star Fleet Project* EP (1983), and recording a solo for Michael Jackson's 'Beat It' (recorded in 1982, released in early '83). Roth was opposed to him sharing his skills, being well aware that Eddie's playing was the band's unique selling point. The incendiary solo helped Jackson's song to become a massive hit and *Billboard* chart-topper, which surely annoyed

Roth, especially when *1984* later peaked at number two, kept off the top spot by *Thriller,* from which 'Beat It' was taken.

Nevertheless, the band commenced work on the album at 5150 studios, with Templeman still producing but Eddie dictating the work rate. The studio's smaller workspace and relatively basic set-up necessitated a new approach. The basic tracks of the band's previous albums were played live together in the studio. In 5150, that wasn't an option. Limited space allowed only Alex and Eddie to record together, with everything else being overdubbed separately. According to Eddie's interview in *Eruption*, the tight space also forced Alex to switch from his full acoustic kit to electronic Simmons drums, with only an acoustic snare to provide his signature sound. Even his cymbals were overdubbed separately due to space and sound-leakage considerations. Fans debate the accuracy of this recollection, with many convinced that the tom sounds on *1984* are acoustic Rototoms, while others swear that all drum sounds on the record are acoustic. The higher toms do indeed sound like Rototoms, but the kick and floor tom sounds are certainly electronic. The slower, more methodical approach dictated by these conditions allowed Eddie more time to pursue his interest in synthesisers, resulting in the band's most keyboard-heavy record to date. Roth, not renowned for his long attention span, was frustrated with the sluggish pace, and had reservations about the synth-led material, but nevertheless turned in some of his finest lyrics and performances. Eventually, the triumphant 'Jump' single was released on 21 December, becoming an instant classic and earning the band a long-deserved US number one.

The album followed on 9 January (in US date conventions, 1/9/84). It had been scheduled for release on New Year's Eve, but Eddie and Donn's desire to make last-minute tweaks to the mix led to a farcical situation involving Landee sneaking out of the studio's back door, hiding the master tapes from an impatient Templeman! When eventually unleashed, packaged in a sleeve featuring an iconic image of an innocent-looking *putto* or cherub sneaking a cigarette, by Margo Nahas, the album quickly became the band's most successful, reaching number two in the US chart and number 15 in the UK. The album's distillation of all things Van Halen – razor-sharp pop hooks, bludgeoning heaviness, proggy complexity and a bucketload of wit and swagger – elicited enthusiastic responses from fans and critics alike. However, the pressure the creative process had placed on the band members' already fractured relationships with one another was great, and something had to give. Although a hugely successful tour followed, it would be years before another Roth-fronted Van Halen record appeared.

'1984' (Van Halen, Van Halen, Roth, Anthony)
More a brief overture than a song in its own right, '1984' prepares the listener for a very different listening experience from previous Van Halen records. Ever since George Orwell's chilling dystopian vision, *Nineteen Eighty-Four (1949),*

the mere mention of the year had carried a sense of futuristic foreboding. This piece played on Eddie's Oberheim OB-Xa (a polyphonic model, much more advanced than the monophonic synths used on earlier releases), reflects these dark associations. The ominous low notes and ethereal chords have echoes of both Vangelis' electronic score to Ridley Scott's dystopian noir *Blade Runner* (1982) and Richard Strauss' orchestral work, *Also Sprach Zarathustra* (1896), famously used in Stanley Kubrik's future nightmare, *2001: A Space Odyssey* (1968). The eerie, sterile coldness gradually softens as the piece goes on, with warmer, major key themes emerging, concluding with a phrase that foreshadows 'Jump', the very next track.

'Jump' (Van Halen, Van Halen, Roth, Anthony)
The keyboard hook of Van Halen's best-known song and biggest hit was composed several years earlier on the electric piano but was vetoed by Roth, who wanted Eddie to stick to the guitar. Seizing the creative reins for *1984*, Eddie reintroduced the idea, now played on the Oberheim OB-Xa, and this time Roth took the bait. His words sound casually thrown together yet provide an instantly memorable hook, simple, engaging narrative, and a dash of upbeat philosophy. The track begins with that famous synth riff: a deep low C pedal note, overlaid with a shifting pattern of major and suspended fourth triads – the same kind of harmonic structure frequently employed in Eddie's guitar riffs. The band enters with a trademark Roth scream and an accented a run of eighth notes from the rhythm section. A rattling Rototom fill introduces a steady, driving beat, with Mike hammering out staccato eighth notes. Dave's vocal line is part-upbeat pop melody, part-ebullient shout, as the first verse espouses a characteristically devil-may-care attitude: 'I get up and nothing gets me down/ You've got it tough? I've seen the toughest around'. The bridge drops to A minor, the tricky rhythm remaining in 4/4 but accented in 3/8 for two bars. Roth circumvents the off-kilter feel with a single-note vocal line in straight eighth notes, gliding smoothly over the turbulent backing. The lyric now becomes a pick-up attempt, placing us in a bar, with our narrator trying to coax us onto the dancefloor from his position leaning by the jukebox: 'Can't you see me standin' here, I've got my back against the record machine/ I ain't the worst that you've seen, can't you see what I mean?'. The chorus hook, with typical gallows humour, was inspired by a news report about a potential suicide considering a leap from a high-rise building. In Dave's lyric, 'Might as well jump' is no longer a suggestion of a fatal plummet, but rather an invitation to leap into life and enjoy the moment – a similar sentiment to 'Dance the Night Away', which goaded us: 'C'mon, take a chance!'.

Given the song's overtly poppy nature, the absence of the band's trademark harmonies is surprising. Instead, the backing vocals simply echo Roth's lead with a rowdy gang yell of 'Jump!' during the chorus. Eddie's guitar is almost inaudible in the verses, playing soft, muted eighth-note chords that blend seamlessly with the synth. He steps out of the shadows in the bridge with a nice melodic arpeggio figure but returns to low-key chugging for the chorus. The instrumental is a separate prog-rock workout within the song, dropping to the unrelated key of B flat minor with more jagged rhythms, breaking up the 4/4 pulse into alternating bars of 3/8 and 5/8. Over this, Eddie plays one of his most iconic solos. It's pieced together from two takes, the first bluesier, with nice use of pinch harmonics, and the second flashier, with explosive tapping, a touch of sweep-picking and a climactic legato ascending run. It's beautifully structured with supple, jazzy phrasing, elevating the song to another level. A keyboard solo follows, consisting of a progression of classical-sounding arpeggios, gradually modulating back to C major for a repeat of the intro. An emphatic extended out-chorus sees Eddie's guitar come up in the mix, and as the song fades, he can be heard playing a muted melodic riff. This fragment, previously heard in occasional live renditions of 'Dance the Night Away', eventually resurfaced in 1991's 'Top of the World'. While most fans wouldn't necessarily consider 'Jump' to be the band's finest moment, it's an undeniably tremendous record, with a cultural reach that far exceeds most of their other work. Coupled with a dynamic performance-based promo video, it cemented the *idea* of Van Halen in the popular consciousness. Their contrasting personalities, energy, power, exuberance and sense of fun all captured at a perfect peak, just before breaking point. In 'Jump', there is no sign of tension or infighting, just sheer uplifting joy.

'Panama' (Van Halen, Van Halen, Roth, Anthony)
The album hits its rock n' roll stride with this hard-driving riff-fest in the vein of 'Everybody Wants Some!'. The relentless momentum and crunching three-chord riff are Eddie's response to the band's request for 'something with an AC/DC beat' according to an interview in *Eruption*. Typically, Roth has given multiple contradictory explanations of the song's lyrics: it's either about a car he saw in a Las Vegas drag race, named 'Panama Express', or his old Opel Kadett station wagon, or a stripper... Irrespective of the original inspiration, the song uses hot rod and drag racing imagery as an extended sexual metaphor, allowing Roth to pile up layers of innuendo. The track begins with a palm-muted riff over a rumble of kick and floor tom, the barely repressed pent-up energy akin to a race car revving on the starting grid. After a minor-key linking section, the band locks into the AC/DC-inspired groove, based around the open chords of E, A and D over Mike's driving low E pedal and Alex's solid 'four on the floor' beat. The AC/DC influence is clear, yet Van Halen's style is looser and more swinging than the lock-step riffing of the Aussie legends. Roth sets the scene, agog as the car/girl of his dreams appears: 'Here she comes, full blast and top down/ Hot shoe, burning down the avenue'. This conjures an image of a speeding convertible, tyres so hot that it leaves flames in its wake. However, it could equally depict the approach of a woman, ala Jayne Mansfield's iconic stroll down the street

Above: The band in 1978, with champagne corks flying as they prepare to take on the world!

Left: Van Halen, captured in a relaxed moment, circa 1991.

Right: A press shot of the 1998 incarnation of the band, with new vocalist Gary Cherone. (*Warner Brothers*)

Left: The iconic cover of the eponymous debut LP, capturing the young band's raw energy. (*Warner Brothers*)

Right: The simple, striking cover of *Van Halen II*, which successfully expanded upon the debut LP's foundations. (*Warner Brothers*)

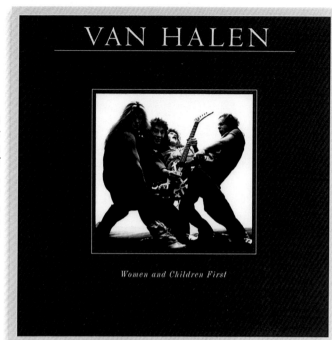

Right: *Women and Children First* stripped away the poppier elements of Van Halen's sound, featuring some of their rawest, heaviest work. (*Warner Brothers*)

Left: Details from The Maze by William Kurelek on the cover of *Fair Warning* reflect the album's dark, turbulent tone. (*Warner Brothers*)

Left: Dave Lee Roth, playing 'Ice Cream Man' on his appropriately ridiculous custom 'Davesickle' guitar.

Right: A young Eddie Van Halen, letting rip on his revolutionary 'Frankenstein' guitar.

Above: Michael Anthony, the relatable everyman with a soaring high tenor voice, and a moderate fondness for Jack Daniels.

Below: Alex Van Halen, a vision in stripes behind one of his trademark gigantic kits.

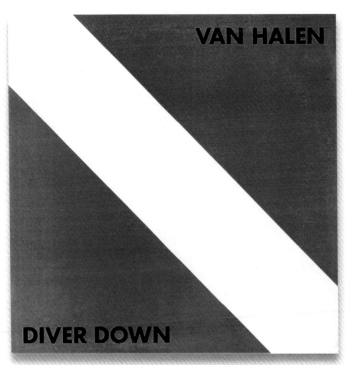

Left: *Diver Down*, a much maligned but thoroughly enjoyable grab-bag of styles and influences. (*Warner Brothers*)

Right: Margo Nahas' painting of a mischievous putto graces the cover of the hugely successful *1984* LP (stylized as *MCMLXXXIV* on the sleeve). (*Warner Brothers*)

Right: Eddie and his diminutive counterpart looking too cool for school in the 'Hot For Teacher' video. (*Warner Brothers*)

Left: Two Daves causing double trouble in the 'Hot For Teacher' video. (*Warner Brothers*)

Right: The boys gamely attempt some dance moves for the 'Hot For Teacher' video. (*Warner Brothers*)

Left: Alex finds himself in a compromising position in the video for 'Panama'. (*Warner Brothers*)

Right: Eddie and Dave, at loggerheads offscreen, share some onstage camaraderie in the 'Panama' video. (*Warner Brothers*)

Left: Incoming! Michael Anthony takes to the sky in the 'Panama' video. (*Warner Brothers*)

Right: Sammy Hagar onstage in the live promo video for 'Dreams', recorded at the Whisky a Go Go in March, 1993. (*Warner Brothers*)

Left: Eddie and Mike share a moment in the 1993 'Dreams' promo. (*Warner Brothers*)

Right: Sammy and Eddie's guitar duel on 'There's Only One Way to Rock', from *Live Without a Net*. (*Warner Brothers*)

Left: A redesigned winged-VH logo held aloft by Atlas on the cover of the first 'Van Hagar' album, *5150*. (*Warner Brothers*)

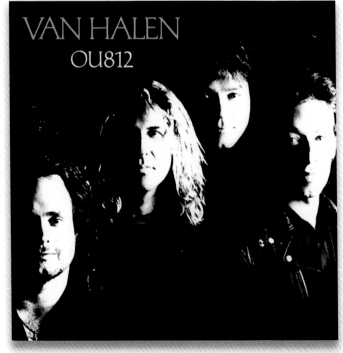

Right: A moodily lit Van Halen stare out pensively from the cover of the patchy-but-enjoyable *OU812*. (*Warner Brothers*)

Right: A bold, simple cover design for the tougher, back-to-basics rock of *For Unlawful Carnal Knowledge*. (*Warner Brothers*)

Left: A photograph of post-tornado devastation in Smyrna, Delaware adorns the cover of *Live: Right here, Right Now*, a very slick, not very 'live' representation of the band's 1992 shows. (*Warner Brothers*)

Left: The cover of 1995's *Balance*, with its warring conjoined twins amid a scorched landscape, seems like a pointed comment on the fractious state of the band at the time. (*Warner Brothers*)

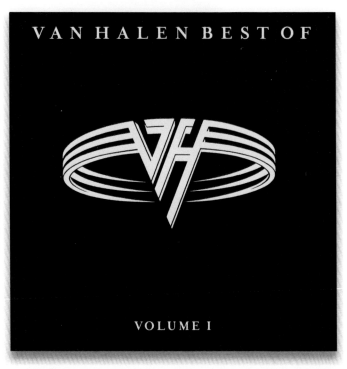

Right: The somewhat-austere cover of *Best of: Volume I*, which perhaps reflects the band's mood in 1996, but undersells the Technicolor delights contained therein! (*Warner Brothers*)

Above: The briefly reunited classic line-up, falling apart before our eyes on the 1996 MTV Video Music Awards. (*MTV*)

Below: Sammy and Eddie onstage during the difficult 2004 tour, which finally ended 'Van Hagar' for good.

Left: Veteran Vaudevillian, Frank Richards takes a cannonball to the stomach on the cover of the ill-fated *Van Halen III*. (*Warner Brothers*)

Right: Eddie's trademark stripes adorn the cover of Van Halen's second compilation, *The Best of Both Worlds*. (*Warner Brothers*)

Right: The classic logo is reinstated on the cover of *A Different Kind of Truth*, a stunning return to form for the reunited band. (*Interscope*)

Left: Van Halen's second live album didn't please everyone, but offered an authentic representation of the 2012 line-up's raw, exciting stage show. (*Warner Brothers*)

Left: Roth in his element, circa 2012.

Right: Father and son united onstage. Wolfgang's presence clearly helped Eddie to find joy in playing with Van Halen again. He was a controversial replacement for Michael, but quickly proved himself worthy.

Left: Roth, the master showman, back in his rightful place, as Alex holds down the beat.

in *The Girl Can't Help It* *(*Frank Tashlin, 1956*)*, leaving a trail of dazzled onlookers, ice melting and milk bottles boiling over in her wake. The line between car and girl becomes more blurred in the fetishistic second verse: 'Ain't nothing like it, her shiny machine/ Got a feel for the wheel, keep the moving parts clean'. And if there's still any doubt about the agenda behind all this car talk, Roth spells it out: 'Got an on-ramp comin' through my bedroom'.

The bridge takes the drag racing imagery further, comparing luring the girl away from another man to winning the prized car in a race for pink slips – a staple challenge of 1950s/60s street racing, referenced in The Beach Boys' 'Little Deuce Coupe' (1963) and the movie *Grease* (1978). 'Don't you know she's coming home with me?', he taunts, 'You'll lose her in the turn, I'll get her!'. The chorus consists of the title sung in burly-sounding unison. After its second appearance, the key changes for a guitar solo which blazes along for eight bars, before settling into a sultry minor-key melody over a hushed two-chord vamp, interspersed with the sound of the revving engine of Eddie's Lamborghini. Dave delivers a memorable mid-song monologue, murmuring suggestively about a late-night drive: 'I can barely see the road for the heat comin' off... reach down between my legs and... ease the seat back'. A series of ascending augmented chords ratchets up the tension, with both music and lyrics edging towards a climax: 'Pistons popping', ain't no stopping now!'. There's cliffhanging pause on the word 'now', with Mike adding the song's only harmony, and then we're into an extended out-chorus. A neat, studio created conclusion sees the backing abruptly cut out, and the last word sung a capella. Accompanied by a high-energy promo video, 'Panama' was released as the album's third single in June 1984 and reached number 13 on the *Billboard* chart. It is one of very few songs to have been performed by every incarnation of the band and remains one of their enduring anthems.

'Top Jimmy' (Van Halen, Van Halen, Roth, Anthony)

This unusual track is Roth's tribute to James Koncek, frontman of R&B combo Top Jimmy and the Rhythm Pigs. Roth had been an enthusiastic patron of the roots rock revival that developed from the late 1970s/early 1980s Hollywood punk scene, frequenting shows, and even helping to bankroll one of his favourite venues, the Zero Zero Club. Along with contemporaries like The Blasters and Los Lobos, the Rhythm Pigs were a popular club draw, with their lairy, drunken takes on blues classics. Roth had guested onstage with the band in 1981, and now took the opportunity to immortalise them in song. In the alternate universe of Roth's narrative, Jimmy and the boys achieve widespread celebrity, while Jimmy himself becomes an unlikely sex symbol! Roth's narrator has been tipped off about a performer who 'sang so good that the roof fell in, and he didn't even stop the show'. This refers to a real-life incident in which the flimsy false ceiling of notorious punk dive, the Cathay de Grande, collapsed during a set by fellow scenesters, The Plimsouls, co-opted by Roth to add to the myth of the Rhythm Pigs. By verse two, the word is out, with 'Jimmy on the television, famous people on there with him, Jimmy on the news at five'. This buzz of excitement is mirrored by the hectic pace of Roth's lyrics, with words crammed into every available space, a syllable to every eighth note. Roth and Anthony harmonise their way through the chorus, concluding that 'Top Jimmy, he's the king!'. Given Dave's justified reputation as a narcissist and self-promoter, it's touching to hear him devote an entire song to mythologising another performer, revealing the depth of his affection for both The Rhythm Pigs, and the scene that spawned them.

The track starts gently, with a music box-like melody, twinkling enigmatically across the stereo spectrum. Eddie played this on a Ripley stereo guitar, designed to allow the player to individually pan each string left or right. This guitar is tuned to an open chord of D5, with an added flattened 7th, allowing Eddie to play the intro melody on natural harmonics. As the track builds, he interjects grungy low chords and overdubs keening volume-swelled divebombs. A careering descending chordal run sets the brisk tempo for the verse, the cleaner tone of the Ripley guitar fittingly steering the feel closer to bar-band R&B than Van Halen's usual heavy rock. Between vocal lines, Eddie plays slippery country/jazz lead runs, recalling the style of Chet Atkins or Les Paul. The instrumental is a complete departure, with the tempo dropping to a weightier half-time stomp as Eddie takes an especially far-out solo, heavy on vibrato bar abuse, coruscating harmonics and wild, polyrhythmic runs, edging towards avant-garde jazz-rock. As the last mangled note warbles off into the void, a slip-sliding riff on the Ripley whisks us back into another verse and chorus. As the final chord rings, Mike and Dave put on their best adoring teenage fan voices to swoon 'Oh, Jimmy!', an amusing conclusion to this charming, freewheeling tribute to the unsung hero of an under-appreciated scene. The extra attention that Van Halen drew to Top Jimmy and The Rhythm Pigs undoubtedly helped their only album, *Pigus Drunkus Maximus,* recorded in 1981, to get a belated release in 1987. Sadly, the band was breaking up by then, and Jimmy himself passed away in 2001. However, Van Halen's song remains as a beacon to guide future generations to this often-overlooked artist and the scene from which he sprang.

'Drop Dead Legs' (Van Halen, Van Halen, Roth, Anthony)

Side one closes with this swaggering rocker, described by Eddie in *Eruption* as 'almost a jazz version of 'Back in Black' (AC/DC, 1980)'. You can see what he means; the spacious crunch of the riff and steady, pounding rhythm have a similar feel to the Aussies' comeback classic. However, the fluid guitar playing and Buddy Rich-like muscular swing of Alex's drums contrast sharply with the no-nonsense rigidity of the Young brothers' approach. The track begins with richly-chorussed open guitar chords before the full band launches into the piledriving main riff. Unusually, this is a three-bar phrase, descending from D to A, via a string of inverted and suspended chords, muted arpeggios and string bends. Roth adds a throaty bellow, his narrator flabbergasted by a passing vision of beauty. The lyric is a simple declaration of extreme horniness, inspired by the iconic scene in Billy Wilder's *Some Like it Hot* (1959) where Jack Lemmon and Tony Curtis lustfully watch Marilyn Monroe's Sugar Kane shimmying down a steam-swathed railway platform, clutching a ukulele case to her bosom. In his book, Dave recalls the formative experience of seeing the film at the age of seven, and deciding, 'I was not only going to be Hercules, I was also going to be Marilyn Monroe.' Years later, speaking to *Spin*, Roth was still fixated, saying: 'I wish I could have been the violin case (*sic*) Marilyn Monroe was carrying in *Some Like it Hot* in the scene where she's walking along the side of the train, with all the smoke and the steam coming out'. The impression the movie made is clear here, as he gleefully yells, 'Dig that steam, giant butt/ Makes me scream!'.

Meanwhile, the band churns out a hypnotic groove with a subtle backing vocal counterpoint. The chorus takes a more melodic direction, with ringing chords and sweet harmonies, before a flashy, fusion-influenced ascending sequence of chords and lead runs brings about a pause. Just as the track seems about to dissipate into vague noodling, Alex crashes back in with a clattering Bonham-esque fill. The second verse and chorus repeat the pattern, building to a climax followed by a pause. However, this time Eddie breaks into a new section, with a funky, muted low-end riff in the left channel, and soft, sustained chords in the right. A third guitar track enters with low-key bluesy phrases, rapidly building in intensity and inventiveness. The remainder of the track is given over to this melodically and rhythmically adventurous solo, containing passages worthy of Alan Holdsworth or Mahavishnu Orchestra/Miles Davis virtuoso John McLaughlin. Though never an A-side, 'Drop Dead Legs' was a B-side twice, on the US release of 'Panama' and the UK single of 'I'll Wait'. It's not the band's most fully realised song, but the terrific Led Zeppelin/AC/DC feel and mind-blowing musicianship make it a favourite of headbangers and guitar nerds alike.

'Hot For Teacher' (Van Halen, Van Halen, Roth, Anthony)
Although Alex has done plenty to earn a place in the pantheon of rock drummers, he tends to be overshadowed by his brother's monumental reputation. There are those, including former manager Noel Monk, who argue that behind Eddie's genius and Dave's showmanship, Alex and Mike were merely competent. Monk alleges in *Runnin' with the Devil* that:

> It didn't matter that Alex wasn't John Bonham or that Michael wasn't John Entwistle. They didn't need to be. They simply had to show up and keep time.

Frankly, this is disingenuous nonsense, as 'Hot for Teacher' amply proves. Alex's intro is legendary among drummers. A fidgety rumble of double kick, building into a thunderous barrage of toms, it's absolutely jaw-dropping.

As this solo settles into a galloping double bass shuffle, Eddie joins with lightning-fast tapped arpeggios. Anthony's bass locks precisely with the relentless kick pulse as Eddie plays a crunching, discordant metallic riff. A sudden halt leaves just Eddie's muted blues picking as Dave – the perennial naughty schoolboy – acts out the first of several vignettes that punctuate the song. Over the classroom hubbub, he asks, 'what do you think the teacher's gonna look like this year?', before a huge drum fill yanks us back into a turbo-charged boogie groove.

Dave's lyrics are another masterpiece of sustained double entendres – a vivid fantasy of inappropriate teacher-student relations that also draws on his own troubled schooldays. The first verse finds the teacher 'screaming' at Roth, perhaps for his cavalier use of double negatives ('don't wanna be no uptown fool')! Our unrepentant protagonist is pleased with himself, noting with eyebrow raised that, 'I'm doing well, teacher needs to see me after school'. The bridge ramps up the innuendo and adds harmonies before the chorus explains our narrator's quandary: 'I've got it bad, I'm hot for teacher!'. The second verse finds Roth getting more mileage from Chuck Berry's 'school/ golden rule' rhyme, previously spotted in 'Fools', and now dripping with salacious double meaning. Between verses, we follow the narrator through his day via more bawdy vignettes. After a blazing solo and Roth's cry of 'class dismissed!', an extended chorus winds up with some jazzy syncopated chords and a crash ending. The track was released as the fourth and final single from *1984*, with an outrageous promo video featuring bikini-clad 'teachers', child actors playing a pint-sized version of Van Halen, and the band in matching suits, attempting Motown-style dance moves! It was the album's least successful single, reaching 56 on the Hot 100, but features near the top of any list of the band's greatest recordings, combining their incredible musicianship, pop sensibility, infectious energy and cheeky humour to tremendous effect. By the next time Van Halen troubled the singles chart, they would be a very different band.

'I'll Wait' (Van Halen, Van Halen, Roth, Anthony, McDonald)

The second single released from *1984*, 'I'll Wait', is close to pure synth-pop, although Alex's warm, chunky snare provides an organic pulse beneath the technological gloss. The song was Van Halen's first to feature input from an outside writer – in this case, Doobie Brothers vocalist/keyboardist Michael McDonald. Roth was struggling for a chorus hook, so Templeman asked McDonald to float some ideas, one of which became what we hear on the finished record. The details of this collaboration have been the subject of controversy. Eddie claimed, in an interview published in *Eruption,* that Templeman secretly recorded McDonald's ideas and surreptitiously passed them to Roth, conspiring to steal them without giving credit. Eddie's adversarial relationship with the singer and producer had become paranoid by this time, colouring his recollection. In truth, the collaboration was open, with no secret tapes. However, it's also true that initial copies didn't credit McDonald, forcing him to resort to legal pressure to ensure his credit was restored. As he told *Ultimate Classic Rock*: 'I guess they thought I was Santa Claus because I had to go chasing them a little bit on that one'.

After an atmospheric minor-key introduction, a rattling Rototom fills brings in the main synth riff. Structured similarly to many of Eddie's guitar riffs, this features a series of chords in their major and sus4 variants over a bass pedal point. The verse reverts to the intro's minor-key feel as a remarkably restrained Roth enters. This unsettling ode begins as a conventional love song, but we soon learn that the object of our narrator's affection isn't someone he knows personally but a girl he's seen in a magazine advertisement with whom he has an entirely imaginary connection. The obsessive tone is reminiscent of The Police's 'Every Breath you Take' (1983), which similarly masks implicit menace behind a seemingly conventional love song. The chorus introduces a hint of threat, with Roth singing, 'I'm coming straight for your heart/ No way you can stop me now'. Mike, not evident on bass, contributes a dramatic high harmony, emphasising the track's minor-key iciness. Verse two finds our narrator realising his obsession is not reciprocated but remaining hopelessly obsessed: 'while she watches, I can never be free – such good photography!'.

A tense synth interlude follows, with Alex playing hi-hat sixteenths and interjecting sonorous fills. Eddie's solo is a tasteful slice of lyrical minor-key blues, his warm, rounded tone adding a welcome human element to the clinical sound. The final phrase spirals off with wild whammy bar vibrato, leading into one more verse. As the final chorus fades, Alex breaks the metronomic pulse with offbeat crashes and accents, concluding this major step towards a more 'mature' sound – something Roth actively resisted. The creepy lyrics complement the music's chilly tone, and the sleek, glossy sound proved successful, reaching number 13 on the *Billboard* Hot 100. However, while state of the art in 1984, it now sounds considerably more dated than the original line-up's more traditional rock material.

'Girl Gone Bad' (Van Halen, Van Halen, Roth, Anthony)
Van Halen's progressive inclinations became more prominent with each album, as Eddie pushed the band's music in more complex directions but were counterbalanced by Roth's pop sensibility. This fine balance often created dazzling moments. If *Diver Down* showed the scales teetering in Dave's favour, 'Girl Gone Bad' finds Eddie firmly taking control. This multipart mini-epic sounds closer to the heavy prog of Rush, circa *Hemispheres* (1978) than Van Halen's signature hard pop. Over a pulsing low A pedal, Eddie builds from gentle tapped harmonics to a chordal fanfare, followed by a passage of jarring, rapid-fire bursts of notes, played in tight unison by drums and guitar, recalling the spectacular jazz-rock flourishes of early King Crimson. The main riff uses A and F chords over the A pedal, with Eddie's

open B and E strings ringing ethereally over the rhythm section's muscular syncopated gallop.

Roth's lyrics hastily sketch the tale of an innocent girl arriving in the big city and becoming a sex worker. There's little detail, but the story is so familiar that the listener can fill in the blanks. Dave's scant eight lines, plus the title repeated for the chorus feel like an afterthought – something to get out of the way so Eddie can concentrate on the serious business of the music. Nevertheless, Dave does his best to make a mark, moaning, wailing, and stepping all over the beat with his languid phrasing. After two minutes, his work is effectively done, and the band veers into an instrumental bridge with a tense stop-time rhythm beneath Eddie's sinuous single-note riff. The ensuing solo is a masterclass in exploratory fusion-inflected shredding, culminating in a tremolo-picked chord sequence, accented in implied 3/8, followed by a reprise of the intro. This time, Eddie adds an exotic augmented fourth to the melodic figure for a subtly unsettling effect. Roth tries to assert his presence in the extended out-chorus while backing vocals add a haunting, high drone. Eddie alternates between driving rhythm and sizzling lead outbursts until Alex's spectacular fills eventually peter out with a bass-drum flurry. As a song, 'Girl Gone Bad' is neither accessible nor catchy, but that's not the point. It's a tremendous showcase for the band's scintillating instrumental interplay and jaw-dropping musicianship.

'House Of Pain' (Van Halen, Van Halen, Roth, Anthony)

Following such a pointedly progressive track, closing the album with a song first demoed in 1976 might seem like a step backwards. Initially, it feels like a return to simple hard rock, with a swaggering, Led Zeppelin-indebted mid-tempo riff. However, while the original song had a conventional structure, the *1984* version jettisons everything except the title and guitar riff, moulding them into an altogether different listening experience. The demo has a strident, metallic feel and a fun, silly horror-themed lyric. By '84, the rhythmic backbone is slower and funkier, and the lyrics' horror imagery has been replaced by references to sadomasochism. These depict a love-hate romantic relationship but could equally be a metaphor for Roth's fractious working relationship with Eddie. Dave's voice is somewhat submerged in the mix and, once again, the vocal portion of the song isn't the main focus. Although he resurfaces to sing along with the outro guitar lick, Dave's work is essentially done by the 1:20 mark, after which the brothers take centre stage.

After the second chorus, there's a brief minor 7th bridge with a wonderfully melodic solo, leading to a dramatic, chromatically ascending chord pattern borrowed from the 1976 original's intro. Eddie's rhythm establishes a new riff – an up-tempo gallop reminiscent of Iron Maiden. An overdubbed solo delivers a maelstrom of slippery legato runs and vertigo-inducing divebombs, eventually easing into a more laid-back bluesy riff. Here, Roth reappears, his husky moan building to a scream as the music's intensity increases. There's some exhilarating interplay between guitar and drums over the fade-out, and Mike sneaks in some nice fills too. 'House of Pain' is among the album's less satisfying tracks in terms of song-craft, but makes an impact by accumulating a series of brilliant, if tenuously related musical set-pieces. Still, it is noticeable that these last two tracks deliberately side-line Roth, emphasising musicianship over charisma. Clearly, something had to change, and over the next year, it certainly did...

5150 (1986)

Personnel:
Sammy Hagar: lead vocals
Edward Van Halen: guitar, keyboards, backing vocals
Michael Anthony: bass, backing vocals
Alex Van Halen: drums
Recorded at 5150 Studios, November 1985 – February 1986
Produced by Mick Jones, Don Landee and Van Halen
Engineered by Don Landee
Record label: Warner Brothers
Release date: 24 March, 1986
Highest chart position: US: 1, UK: 16
Running time: 43:14
Current edition: Rhino Records CD reissue

1984 took Van Halen to new commercial heights, selling huge numbers of records and spawning a string of mainstream hit singles with memorable promo videos, extending the band's reach far beyond their core rock audience. The *1984* tour was their biggest to date, but by its conclusion, the band was at breaking point. One source of bitterness was the issue of songwriting royalties. Since their recording career began, the band had divided writing credits and revenue evenly between themselves, irrespective of individual contributions. However, although arrangements were often collaborative, it was almost always Eddie alone who composed the backing music, with Dave adding the melody and lyrics, also unassisted. As sales grew, and royalty earnings became more substantial, this even-handedness began to seem unfair to the principal writers. As Eddie's brother and principal musical foil, Alex was exempt from criticism, so Mike bore the brunt of his bandmates' ire. Accordingly, he was pressured into signing an agreement to receive no further writing royalties from the recently released *1984*, or from any future Van Halen records, souring the atmosphere within the band.

Furthermore, irked by Eddie's numerous outside projects and frustrated by the increasingly slow, laborious process of recording with Van Halen, Roth decided to indulge in some projects of his own, starting with a solo EP, *Crazy from the Heat* (1985). Consisting of four covers, allowing Roth to exercise the campy, showbiz tendencies which were increasingly unwelcome in Van Halen, it gave him two hit singles. Although Roth's bandmates publicly supported this venture, seeing the singer succeeding alone must have needled Eddie. Annoyance became serious concern as Dave made plans to direct and star in a film based on his own screenplay, also titled *Crazy from the Heat*. Roth, a lifelong movie nut, had directed promo videos, and was keen to transition to the big screen. CBS studios offered him a $10m budget and he was raring to go. Meanwhile, work on the follow-up to *1984* progressed slowly and unsatisfactorily. According to Roth's autobiography, 'There were constant delays and screaming. It sounded like a sack of sick cats. And that's what rehearsal was like. That's what trying to write the songs was like'. Roth was dismayed by the 'melancholy power ballads' Eddie was writing, and with the album not ready, suggested a summer tour, to keep the band in the public eye. Eddie felt the movie had become Roth's main priority, and that he lacked commitment to the new album, preferring to make easy money on the road. Things finally boiled over in a tearful meeting that March, and suddenly, Roth was no longer a member of Van Halen.

Although his movie fell through after CBS dissolved their film division, Roth was quick to regroup. With the EP having established his solo credentials, he assembled a crack squad of musicians and started work on his own LP with Ted Templeman producing. Meanwhile, numerous potential Van Halen vocalists were suggested and rejected. At one point, the idea of making a record featuring a different guest singer on each track was floated; at other times, the depressed band wondered if they could continue at all without Roth. In the end, the solution was unexpectedly provided by Eddie's car dealer, Claudio Zampolli. Eddie had brought his Lamborghini for a service and was admiring a Ferrari that another customer had dropped off. Zampolli mentioned that the car belonged to former Montrose frontman and current solo star Sammy Hagar, and suggested that Eddie call him. Hagar went along to jam with the band, and despite misgivings about their chaotic, hard-drinking lifestyle, found he had immediate musical and personal chemistry with them. Against his better judgement, Hagar put his solo career on hold, becoming the lead singer of Van Halen.

Work on *5150* commenced in November 1985 at Eddie's studio, after which the record would be named. With Templeman out of the picture, his erstwhile partner Donn Landee stepped into the producer role. Foreigner's Mick Jones co-produced, following Hagar's concerns that Landee lacked production experience. *5150* has a markedly glossier, more 'produced' feel than the previous records, with extensive overdubbing and more synths. Eddie's sound is different, partly due to his newly-acquired Steinberger guitar, which featured a then-revolutionary 'TransTrem' unit – a vibrato system which kept the guitar's strings in tune with one another as the overall pitch was lowered or raised and enabled the player to lock the unit in pre-set positions, changing the guitar's tuning mid-song. Alex's drums sounded different too. Although his snare still had its classic woody 'thwack', the rest of his recording set-up was now entirely electronic Simmons drums. A popular sound in the mid-eighties, their artificial tone immediately time-stamps any recording on which they feature.

While the Roth/Van Halen partnership had hinged on the tension between two wildly different individuals, Eddie and Sammy were very much on the same page as one another, at least initially. Several years older than his new bandmates, Hagar was a veteran performer and a true professional, without the prima donna attributes that made Roth both entertaining to watch and maddening to work with. Additionally, he was more musician than a showman, and as an accomplished guitarist, could communicate musically with Eddie in a way that Roth could not. Despite the band's chaotic lifestyle, recording generally went well, with the album completed in February 1986 and released the following month. The cover image depicted an Atlas figure carrying a gigantic metal sphere on his shoulders, emblazoned with a modified version of the classic 'winged VH' logo. Preceded by the catchy 'Why Can't This be Love?' single, the album immediately went to number one on the *Billboard* chart, becoming their best-performing record to date – a massive vindication for the band after many had predicted failure without their iconic frontman.

Reviews were a mixed bag. Inevitably, critics who appreciated Roth's witty, characterful grandstanding were unimpressed by Hagar's earnest journeyman approach. Nevertheless, most agreed that, whatever the singers' relative merits, the musical spark was still there, and if some disapproved of the overtly radio-friendly sound, it was undeniably phenomenally commercially successful. Listening now, production choices that seemed cutting edge in 1985 have aged poorly, much more so than their earlier records. Hagar is technically more accomplished than Roth, with a bigger range and a classic gravelly blues-rock tone. However, Roth's expressiveness, flair and wit that are sorely missed on the Hagar-era records. That said, *5150* is a fine album, blending adventurous heavy rock with slick, highly commercial AOR to create an unstoppable stadium-filling behemoth.

'Good Enough' (Van Halen, Van Halen, Hagar, Anthony)

The first album by 'Van Hagar' (as the reconfigured band was inevitably nicknamed) opens with Sammy's lecherous cry of 'Hello baaaaby!', cribbed from the Big Bopper's 1958 novelty, 'Chantilly Lace'. With a whinnying harmonic squeal and a rattling kick-and-floor tom flam, the band launches into a solid mid-tempo riff. Eddie's sound, though still recognisable, is more processed, closer to the tones favoured by contemporary metal acts than the warm, natural feel we're used to. He emphasises the metallic edge by tuning his low E string all the way down to A, allowing him to play chords in the normal register on the other five strings while maintaining a guttural, doomy chug on the low A. Hagar's full-throated bluesy roar enters, interspersed with bursts of scattershot harmonics and yowling divebombs. It's an authoritative vocal debut that effectively showcases his leather-lunged power. His lyrics, on the other hand... Cretinous sexism was common in 1980s rock lyrics, Roth's included. However, even at his crudest, Dave's words are tempered with self-aware humour and a balancing hint of self-deprecation. Hagar, by contrast, leans towards outright witless misogyny, as 'Good Enough' demonstrates. This not-at-all veiled ode to cunnilingus starts by literally describing a woman's anatomy as a piece of meat ('U.S prime grade A stamped, guaranteed/ Grease it up and turn on the heat') and gets worse from there!

There's a brief chord change to D at the end of the verse, and Alex unleashes a big fill, before the chorus returns to chugging along in A, although a nifty, slippery high guitar melody and Michael's high harmony break the monotony. After the second chorus, the band kicks into stomping double time for a booming riff on that low A string, uncomfortably similar to the central riff of Yes's 'Owner of a Lonely Heart' (1983). The instrumental that follows is a highlight, with Eddie's blazing solo played over a new melancholic section in unusual 6/4 time. A wolf whistle from Hagar ushers in a spoken vignette featuring the singer 'hilariously' sexually harassing a waitress. This obvious attempt at Roth-like knockabout spontaneity falls woefully flat. Hagar is a fine singer but lacks the charm or charisma to carry off such nonsense. The Yes-alike riff returns, now with a catchy high backing vocal, briefly creating the impression of a monstrously-heavy Motown girl group! The final verse is improved by the addition of a gospel-like call-and-response structure, with harmony vocals echoing back the end of each line. The track ends with a spectacular guitar cadenza and a piercing scream. Although 'Good Enough' is solid, it feels stodgy and uninspired compared to the dizzying heights of *1984*. Additionally, the transparent attempts to recreate Roth's irreverent energy feel forced and inevitably fall flat. It's not terrible but sounds like a band trying to recapture their past, rather than discovering their future.

'Why Can't This Be Love' (Van Halen, Van Halen, Hagar, Anthony)

Track two is a stronger statement of intent for the Hagar-fronted band. Not quite a ballad, it nevertheless showcases a lovelorn melancholia that Roth would have rejected but at which Hagar excels. Commencing with an irresistible bubbling synth riff, played on Eddie's Oberheim OB-8, it settles into a steady mid-tempo rhythm, with tasteful power chords providing some background rock muscle. Alex's chunky snare packs its usual punch, but Anthony's playing is buried beneath thrumming synth bass. The verse drops into a pensive minor key, as Hagar emotes about 'that funny feeling again'. The premise is simple: he loves the girl and sees potential for a relationship, but she's less convinced. Sammy's words have been the subject of mockery, especially the second verse's clumsy assertion that 'only time will tell if we stand the test of time'. However, tautology aside, it's a perfectly functional lyric, matching the music's tone well, without the uncomfortable crassness that marred 'Good Enough'. There's little wit or nuance to 'Straight from the heart, oh tell my why can't this be love', but sung with un-Roth-like sincerity over a nagging synth hook, it's the stuff that radio playlists and stadium singalongs are made of.

The bridge allows a prog/fusion influence to surface as Sammy scats along with Eddie's offbeat arpeggio-based guitar/synth melody, showcasing his impressive upper range. It's a hint of adventurousness delivered in a catchy, palatable form. The guitar solo is harmonically darker but surprisingly restrained – a chord-based melody with a little whammy bar ornamentation, blending with the squelching synth. After a reprise of the scat bridge, an extended chorus lets Hagar showcase more impressive upper register work. In some ways, the song is a natural next step from 'Jump', yet its simple romantic, melancholic tone marks a clear departure from the Roth years. The single, released in March 1986, was a great success, reaching number three on the *Billboard* Hot 100 and number eight in the UK. The 12" single included an unnecessarily padded five-minute mix of the song, but the 'proper' album version remains a compact, perfectly constructed slice of stadium pop.

'Get Up' (Van Halen, Van Halen, Hagar, Anthony)

If the previous track showed the band's mellower side, 'Get Up' finds them in obnoxiously aggressive form. Co-producer Mick Jones told *Guitar World*: 'I'd never heard anything like it in my life. It sounded like four guys fighting inside the speaker cabinets, beating the shit out of each other'. It opens with a lone guitar, Eddie smashing out power chords with a snarling, metallic tone and using the TransTrem to move whole chords with lurching violence. As the intro's last note feeds back, Alex launches a full-throttle thrash metal-like double-kick assault. While the band's fastest numbers had previously been shuffles, rooted in 1970s blues/boogie rock, 'Get Up' eschews swing for pulverising forward momentum, reflecting changing trends in heavy music. Alex's performance is relentlessly energetic and inventive but is hindered by the artificial sound of the Simmons drums, which sits awkwardly in the mix. The main riff is a savage, slashing affair. Eddie uses the TransTrem to veer precariously between chords for a slide guitar-like effect, before reining things in, providing tight syncopated stabs behind Hagar's gut-busting vocal. As with 'Good Enough', there's little melody – just basic blues-scale wailing. The lyric is a tough-love attempt to shake a friend out of relationship-related doldrums, urging them to 'Get up and make it work'. To match the harsh music, Hagar strikes a brusque, unsympathetic tone, bellowing, 'You say that love has got you down, well that's bullshit'. Charming! Otherwise, it's a steady stream of well-worn cliches ('Hold your head up high, look them in the eye, never say die'), but delivered with admirable conviction. The chorus is rather perfunctory, but gains punch from Mike's high harmony. The instrumental provides a reflective interlude amidst the racket, with a soft chordal melody over a soft snare shuffle. As the volume is cranked back up, a second guitar bursts in, playing neo-classical tapped arpeggios over a surprisingly pretty chord progression before spiralling away as the chorus returns. After a pointless reprise of the first verse and another chorus, the song ends on an especially over-the-top stadium rock blowout, with Mike and Sammy both screaming at the top of their registers while Eddie wreaks sonic havoc – a fittingly bombastic conclusion to this enjoyably unsubtle track.

'Dreams' (Van Halen, Van Halen, Hagar, Anthony)

A sleek rush of quintessentially mid-eighties soft rock, 'Dreams' is a favourite of many Hagar-era fans. It opens with a saccharine synth melody, doubled on acoustic guitar, oozing a sentimentality that would have been unthinkable from the Roth-era band. Thankfully, the rhythm section provides a solid, rocking backbone, and a piano sound is blended with the synth for a fuller, more organic feel. Aside from tasteful snippets of lead, Eddie's guitar chugs unobtrusively, submerged in the mix. The verse drops to a minor key, matching the bleak scene Hagar paints: 'World turns black and white/ Pictures in an empty room'. The song suggests we combat this negativity with a string of motivational cliches: 'reach for the sky', 'spread your wings' etc. The bridge returns to the uplifting major, with Hagar urging us 'higher and higher', and the melody following suit, pushing him to the top of his impressive range. This reinforces the soaring feel of the track, although the lung-bursting exertion required to hit such improbable notes leaves little room for nuanced expression. In live performances, Mike would sing the second 'higher' to allow Sammy to draw a much-needed breath! After the second verse, the beat pauses, save for dramatic floor tom accents, as Sammy belts out the chorus melody over the syrupy synth/acoustic motif from the intro. The song takes a sharp left turn into the instrumental. Over a menacing power chord riff, Eddie unleashes a flowing solo, replete with pinging harmonics, smooth legato runs, and an obvious splice before the final tapped section. After another bridge and chorus, Eddie's lead doubles the synth melody with a smooth, singing tone, before a final tag chorus concludes that 'In the end, on dreams we will depend/ Oh that's what love is made of', an observation that strives for profundity while being completely meaningless.

In fairness to Sammy, cliches become cliches because people love them and want to keep hearing them. If some listeners missed Roth's storytelling and wit, many more loved Hagar's accessible, relatable style, discussing simple themes in broad strokes and familiar language. 'Dreams' is the antithesis of everything the Roth-era band stood for, but it's an effective and affecting song of its type, showing how quickly and successfully Van Halen had morphed into a soft rock powerhouse. The band chose not to make any promo videos for the album, so Warners cobbled together some footage of the Blue Angels aerial display team to accompany 'Dreams' – a corny but effective decision, reflecting the lyrics' 'higher and higher' hook, and cashing in on the popularity of films like *Top Gun* (Tony Scott, 1986) and *Iron Eagle* (Sidney J. Furie, also 1986) which successfully married high-octane jet action with pop-rock soundtracks. The single reached number 22 on the Hot 100 and went on to become a staple of classic rock radio. Sammy himself was particularly proud of the song, continuing to perform it throughout his post-Van Halen solo career

'Summer Nights' (Van Halen, Van Halen, Hagar, Anthony)
This ready-made summer anthem was the first song Hagar worked on with Van Halen, prior to joining. The band had been up all night, writing and

drinking, when Sammy arrived at 5150. As he recalls in his autobiography, *Red: My Uncensored Life in Rock*:

> We started playing, and the engineer Donn Landee recorded everything we did. I made up the first line on the spot – 'Summer nights and my radio.' It just popped into my head the first time I heard that riff.

The song they wrote together is a highlight of the Van Hagar years, with a huge three-chord riff and a massive singalong chorus. It's a fun, nostalgic evocation of male adolescence, in the tradition of The Beach Boys' 'I Get Around' and 'All Summer Long' (both 1964) and Thin Lizzy's 'The Boys are Back in Town' (1976), with some complex musical ideas concealed behind the sunny, accessible façade. The track opens with a finger-picked chordal guitar melody, folky sounding but for the heavily overdriven tone used. A grunt from Sammy heralds the main riff – big ringing open-position chords, the spaces between phrases filled with lightning-fingered runs and slashing pick slides. Eddie makes full use of the TransTrem to navigate several key changes, audibly dropping his tuning by three semitones just before the drums come in. The verse moves from bright, poppy D major to bluesy B, with Eddie weaving syncopated riffs around the vocal. A brief bridge ramps up tension with a chromatically ascending bassline and double-kick flurries. The chorus is a triumph of simplicity – three chords, an instantly hummable melody and a relatable lyric: 'We celebrate when the gang's all here/ Hot summer nights, you're my time of the year'. Mike's magnificent high harmony is the magic ingredient, elevating this from merely catchy to truly special. After the second chorus, the track suddenly veers into a spooky instrumental in implied C minor, with jazzy E flat 9th and D9th chords mixed in. The ensuing solo is positively avant-garde, abandoning conventional notions of rhythm and key so completely that, in order to get back to the song, the track completely halts and resets with a reprise of the intro. This takes us to an extended out-chorus, with Sammy ad-libbing over bright harmonies, and Eddie adding a chiming harmonic melody over the fade.

The lyrics contain some crass sexism ('Me and the boys wanna play some love with the little human toys'. Urgh!), and Sammy's plan to spend his summer evening 'hanging around near the local parking lot' doesn't sound terribly appealing! Nevertheless, the chorus creates a warm glow of nostalgia, and the second verse's assertion that 'next year I'll head out for the coast' adds a hint of poignancy – this may be the last, perfect summer before everything changes. It's a quintessential coming-of-age moment, combined with some particularly anthemic rock to make a sure-fire classic. It was released as the B side of 'Love Walks In' in July 1986 and also pressed as a promotional twelve-inch single, climbing to number 33 on the *Billboard* Mainstream Rock chart, which is based on airplay rather than sales.

'Best Of Both Worlds' (Van Halen, Van Halen, Hagar, Anthony)

This mid-tempo rocker is the track on *5150* that comes closest to the Roth-era sound. The simple, powerful riff is, bizarrely, reminiscent of the one from Kool and the Gang's 'Celebration' (1980), albeit delivered in the manner of AC/DC. The track is uncomplicated but effective, with bold, dynamic shifts between the verses' soft broken chords and the blasting chorus. The straightforward, blues-based melody is comfortable territory for Hagar, and Mike's harmonies again contribute greatly to a memorable chorus hook. Although the guitar solo moves into a different key, it's a natural continuation of the track, rather than a detour into the unknown, as Eddie blends languorous sustain with bursts of legato speed and zippy tapped fretboard glissandos, before falling back into a quiet reiteration of the riff. Over this, Hagar sings another verse, and then skips the bridge for an extended final chorus.

Lyric-wise, the song's message is clear: rather than waiting for an idealised afterlife, use the time you have to create 'a little heaven right here on earth'. Hagar is at his best with this kind of broad concept, expressed in accessible terms, which, if lacking poetry or nuance, makes for a great shout-along chorus. He only loses his way slightly when attempting something more artful. The second verse describes 'a picture in a gallery/ Of a fallen angel, looked a lot like you', referring to a painting in the Louvre, which he was convinced depicted his mother in a past life. Hagar's fascination for mystical, new-age ideas sometimes seeps into his lyrics which, viewpoint-depending, may add depth to a song or render it nonsensical. Personally, I prefer his lyrics to remain more grounded, as they thankfully do for most of this track. Released as the album's fourth single, the song failed to trouble the Hot 100 but became a live favourite, with good reason.

'Love Walks In' (Van Halen, Van Halen, Hagar, Anthony)

When, in his autobiography, Roth attributes his departure from the band to his desire not to 'commit poetic felonies, wind up doing melancholy power ballads', he could have been referring to 'Love Walks In'. Opening with a cloyingly lush keyboard melody, using the same synth/ piano blend as 'Dreams', the song ticks every box on the AOR ballad checklist: earnest, angsty minor-key verses with a plodding pedal-point bassline, a soaring, twinkling major-key chorus replete with dramatic cymbal swells, a rocking-yet-tastefully-restrained guitar solo... It's a well-executed, effective product, appealing to listeners far beyond the band's core rock audience and reaching number 22 in the Hot 100. However, it's scarcely recognisable as Van Halen, sounding closer to the work of mega-successful 1980s songwriters like Diane Warren or Desmond Child.

The lyrics make the odd choice of using the idea of possession by extra-terrestrial beings to discuss the disorienting effects of new love, introducing mystical, arcane elements to an otherwise middle-of-the-road commercial love song. According to *Red,* the song was inspired by Journalist-turned-mystic Ruth Montgomery's book *Aliens Among Us* (1985):

> The book was about walk-ins, aliens who come and take over your body in your sleep. A person can actually not die and still become a whole different person. They wake up one morning and can't remember who the hell they were.

This leads to some peculiar lyrics, such as the chorus' assertion that 'some kind of alien waits for the opening and simply pulls a string'. The song progresses further into science fiction territory until, by verse three, our narrator has been abducted, taken 'far across the Milky Way' by his alien overlords. Whether this seems profound or mere banal nonsense depends on the individual's attitude towards new-age mysticism. It's not for me, but 'Love Walks In' sold a lot of records, and remains a fan favourite, so what do I know? Incidentally, this is one of several songs for which, on early Van Hagar tours, Eddie would move to keyboard, leaving Sammy to handle guitar duties – another big change from how the band functioned during the Roth years.

'5150' (Van Halen, Van Halen, Hagar, Anthony)
The album's title track is the only one to really show the band's progressive side. It begins with a tuneful riff based around palm-muted broken chords, soon joined by snare and hi-hat. A big drum fill introduces the full band, the riff moving to lower-register open chords that ring over a pedal note. The verse has a half-time feel, with a chugging riff in sludgy drop-D tuning. The pace picks back up in the bridge, with a skippy, syncopated kick drum pattern and angelic background vocal 'ooohh's. A brief instrumental rocks the boat with a series of fiendish modulations and unexpected accents before the main riff returns, catapulting us into the upbeat chorus. A tense, urgent minor-key riff accompanies the guitar solo. Eddie stretches out, building from terse, choked bends through elaborate tapped passages and whammy bar tricks to a tremolo-picked climax. Alex matches the increasing intensity of Eddie's lines with bursts of rapid-fire double kick, noticeably increasing in speed. A pause at the solo's conclusion allows the band to reset the tempo as they reprise the introduction before a final chorus extends into a fade, with huge-sounding harmonies on the 'I'll meet you half the way' refrain.

Hagar's lyrics depict an attempt to find the middle ground in a fraught relationship. The title reflects the theme of uneven compromise: the narrator wants to meet his partner 'half the way', but she's 'never satisfied', always craving 'one more'. Hence, instead of a 50/50 relationship, it's a 51/50 arrangement. It's one of Sammy's better lyrics, with fun wordplay and some nice turns of phrase. Add a breezy pop melody, which belies the musical complexity lurking beneath, and you've got something that feels like classic Van Halen. Although the singles are by far the best-known songs on *5150*, for me, the title track is easily the album's highlight, showing what the reconfigured band could do when they steered away from the middle of the road.

'Inside' (Van Halen, Van Halen, Hagar, Anthony)

The album ends with this loose funk rock novelty. Built on a relentless bass synth riff, clearly indebted to the clavinet part from Led Zeppelin's 'Trampled Under Foot' (1975), it takes a broad satirical peek behind the curtain of the music industry, showing us 'what's coming down on the inside'. Hagar portrays a jaded industry veteran who abandoned his individuality to succeed, saying, 'It's not who you are, you see, it's how you dress'. He still craves 'some brand-new groove to sink my teeth into', but instead spends his time 'sitting around just getting high'. Eddie's guitar feels loose and improvisatory, which may account for its marginalised place in the mix, panned hard right while the synth bass takes centre stage. Throughout, the band's banter simulates the boozy, gossipy hubbub of an industry gathering. This strives for the spontaneous fun of the Roth-era but feels self-conscious, with a sense of strained, hollow zaniness. On the plus side, the spoken non-sequiturs provide a distraction from the undercooked song, which despite a blazing guitar solo and spirited turn from Hagar, is an unfinished afterthought.

The band seem unsure of their direction, trying to compensate for the absence of Roth, rather than fully embracing their new identity. Their confidence would be bolstered by the success of *5150*, especially after Roth's 1985 debut LP couldn't match it commercially. On their first tour, the new line-up made a clear break with their past, playing only three Roth-era songs and padding the set with tunes from Hagar's solo records. The new band was establishing an identity which would be fully realised by their next release.

OU812 (1988)

Personnel:
Sammy Hagar: lead vocals, rhythm guitar
Edward Van Halen: guitar, keyboards, backing vocals
Michael Anthony: bass, backing vocals
Alex Van Halen: drums
Recorded at 5150 Studios, September 1987 – April 1988
Recorded by Don Landee
Record label: Warner Brothers
Release date: 24 May 1988
Highest chart position: US: 1, UK: 16
Running time: 50:09
Current edition: Rhino Records CD reissue

Following the success of *5150* and its accompanying tour, Van Halen were keen to keep up their momentum and get to work on new material. However, there were a couple of pressing matters to be taken care of before that could happen. Firstly, following an intervention shortly after the tour concluded, Alex checked into rehab, finally addressing his self-destructive drinking and committing to a sober existence. Meanwhile, although Sammy was recording for Warners with Van Halen, he still owed a solo album to Geffen. Enlisting Eddie to co-produce and play bass, Sammy cut *I Never Said Goodbye* in a mere ten days. It was released in June 1987, rising to number 14 on the *Billboard* chart. Making the next Van Halen record was a considerably more time-consuming process, with recording commencing in September 1987 and concluding in April the following year. While Templeman had always ensured everything stayed on schedule and under budget, *OU812* was recorded at 5150 with the band and Landee handling production duties between them without outside help, making for a much less disciplined approach.

The album they produced is musically wider-ranging than its predecessor, showing the band relaxing with each other, stretching out and experimenting. Conversely, perhaps because of this laid-back approach, it feels less focused than *5150*. In *Eruption*, Eddie recalls it fondly, saying, 'That album wasn't heavy metal or hard rock – it was just a good diverse rock and roll album'. In *Red,* Sammy voices more mixed feelings, claiming that Alex's playing 'wasn't as good' when sober, and acknowledging that 'The songs were not my best stuff lyrically'. Contemporary reviews were similarly ambivalent, but that didn't prevent the album from climbing straight to the US number one spot, and producing a string of top forty hits, continuing Van Hagar's winning streak.

The title, in the concise, numerical tradition of *1984* and 5150, was apparently spotted on the side of a delivery truck but inevitably invited speculation that it was intended as a riposte to Roth's 1986 LP, *Eat 'Em and Smile*. The packaging was austere, featuring a moodily-lit monochrome shot of the band on the cover, a nod to The Beatles' sophomore UK album, *With*

The Beatles. The rear cover features a similarly-lit photo of Hugo Rheinhold's sculpture, *Ape with Skull* (circa 1893), which depicts a chimpanzee contemplating a human skull while sitting on a stack of books, including a volume of Darwin's writings and a bible – atypical artwork material for a late-eighties hard rock record, but apposite to the theme of opening track, 'Mine All Mine'. In 1988, the music industry had a vested interest in promoting compact discs, with their long run-time and huge profit margin, as the premium music format. To encourage buyers, labels urged artists to produce extended versions of their albums for the CD release. Van Halen followed suit on *OU812*, adding a version of Little Feat's 'A Apolitical Blues', as a bonus for digital listeners – the first cover the band had recorded since *Diver Down*. That album included a performance by Jan Van Halen, who sadly passed away in late 1986, and to whom *OU812* is dedicated.

'Mine All Mine' (Van Halen, Van Halen, Hagar, Anthony)

For a band primarily associated with good-time rock, 'Mine All Mine' is a bold opener. Over music owing more to Marillion or early-eighties Genesis than it does to classic Van Halen, Sammy's lyrics describe a quest for spiritual fulfilment, his narrator encountering different religions and philosophies, only to find them all lacking. His eventual solution is to 'stop lookin' out, start lookin' in' – finding insight within himself rather than turning to others for answers. The lyric posed a major challenge for Hagar, who told journalist Marin Popoff in an interview posted on *martinpopoff.com*:

> I rewrote that song lyrically seven times. And it was the last song I did vocals on for the record. I wouldn't sing it because I was unsure about my lyrics and wasn't really confident about what I was trying to say.

The effort was worthwhile, as 'Mine All Mine' is one of Hagar's better lyrics. Granted, it's heavy-handed in places, but overall, it's a strong, coherent piece of writing, leading the listener through spiritual angst to a bright, self-empowering conclusion. It's more intelligent and less hackneyed than any lyrics from *5150* and vastly superior to that LP's risible opener, 'Good Enough'.

Rolling Stone's David Fricke called the song 'a good teaser for the future', but ironically, it's one of the band's most dated-sounding tracks now, thanks to the very eighties pop-prog synths that dominate throughout. The track opens with a gritty, menacing synth bass line, doubled by an overdriven guitar, while another cleaner, chorused guitar plays choppy chords and a gently strummed enigmatic D minor 9th. Alex plays up a storm, keeping steady eighth notes on his kick drums while hitting off-kilter snare accents, belying Hagar's negative assessment of his sober playing. The artificial drum sounds of *5150* are gone too, making for a much less jarring listening experience. The dark, troubled-sounding pattern underpinning the verses gives way to a more upbeat major-key bridge. The chorus sees the clouds part, with the thunderous beat subsiding, and angelic harmonies emerging. In the instrumental the guitar comes to the forefront with a solo that reflects the narrator's spiritual journey, moving through turbulent minor-key angst to conclude with a bold, melodic major-key phrase. After a final verse and chorus, we return to the brooding intro riff, with Hagar ad-libbing until the track is suddenly cut off, leaving the final 'Mine, all mine' unaccompanied. It's a brave, unusual choice for an album opener, but it pays off. Even if the now-dated keyboard sounds have a time-capsule effect, it's a powerful, exciting track, proving that Van Hagar could really deliver when they put their minds to it.

'When It's Love' (Van Halen, Van Halen, Hagar, Anthony)

Unfortunately, following the thrilling tempest of 'Mine All Mine', the album sails into the soft rock doldrums with this particularly sappy ballad. The guitar/synth riff and the verses have a little bluesy raunch to them, albeit in the bland, airbrushed manner of 1980s Eric Clapton, but the main synth figure, which also underpins the chorus, is pure saccharine. Using a blend of lush strings and twinkling electric piano sounds, it's the kind of sickly mush that also propelled Richard Marx and Michael Bolton into the charts during this era. Sammy's lyrics return to nondescript banality, taking two verses and an endlessly repeated chorus to tell us that people spend their lives looking for love. How will they know when they've found it, Sammy? 'I can't tell you, but it lasts forever'. Very helpful! Speaking to Popoff, Sammy proudly recalled that the brothers played the song's music to him during a drive from the airport, and 'by the time we got to the studio, that song was written and done, lyrics, melody, everything'. One can't help but wish he'd spent a little more time on it, as although Sammy strains to inject emotional depth, there's no substance behind the slick bombast.

There are some redeeming characteristics, of course. Alex's drums are punchy and virile, rescuing us from total wuss-rock oblivion, and Eddie's solo has a tastefully refined bluesiness. Mike's harmonies are terrific as ever, and Hagar's vocal is also strong, although his tendency towards hernia-inducing screeching high notes is off-putting. Still, though well performed and slickly produced, 'When It's Love' is vacuous at heart – a cynical exercise in power ballad box-ticking. Of course, countless fans of the Hagar era will strongly disagree. The song is undeniably popular, the single reaching number 5 on the *Billboard* Hot 100 and number 28 in the UK in June 1988, and in 2003, was ranked 24th in VH1's list of the 25 greatest power ballads of all time, so what do I know?

'A.F.U (Naturally Wired)' (Van Halen, Van Halen, Hagar, Anthony)

After all that schmaltz, 'A.F.U (Naturally Wired)' is a welcome return to guitar-based rock. It's not the most coherent song – more a patched-together collection of ideas than a complete, well-developed concept – but it's a welcome return to the terrific ensemble playing with which the band made their name. Eddie and Alex both let loose, and Mike even sneaks in some nice bass runs – a rarity for an LP on which his playing is often barely audible. Never one to reject the most obvious idea, Hagar responds to the band's blistering rock n' roll with a lyric about... playing some blistering rock n' roll, revelling in ludicrous heavy metal cliches all the way. There's a strong whiff of Spinal Tap to lyrics like 'Through the ice into the fire, blowin' steam/ North and south, east and west, right and left, I'm always extreme', although Sammy's performance is so overblown, it just about works.

Really though, this track is all about the band's blazing instrumental prowess. From Alex's revving drum intro and Eddie's tapped harmonic melody to the barrelling momentum and lithe fluidity of the main riff, it's a bravura performance. The smouldering, ominous drone of the verse riff erupts into the belting, up-tempo bridge and chorus through a tense, jarring prog-metal interlude, and into an explosive solo. The breathless energy and momentum are such that you barely notice the chaotic structure or the absence of much of a song to hold it all together. It's hardly their most essential track, but still, a welcome reminder of the raw power Van Halen can muster when they drop the plasticky corporate rock trappings of their more chart-friendly material.

'Cabo Wabo' (Van Halen, Van Halen, Hagar, Anthony)

Inspired by the Mexican city of Cabo San Lucas, this swaggering rocker is a natural successor to 'Summer Nights', with its potent blend of strident riffs, pounding, Zeppelin-esque drums, escapist lyrics and big pop hooks. Hagar owned a house in Cabo and retreated there to work on his lyrics. While there, the sight of an inebriated local attempting to make his way home in the early hours sparked an idea. Christening the man's drunken wobble, the 'Cabo Wabo', Sammy composed a lyric comparing the potency of the local mescal and tequila with the intoxicating aura of Cabo San Lucas itself. In Sammy's vision, the drunkard's totter is a dance (you can 'do the Cabo Wabo' like the Twist or the Watusi), and if you fall flat on your face, it's because you're 'kissing the ground'. As a framework, Hagar used his old song, 'Make it Last', from Montrose's self-titled 1973 debut. Upon returning to the US, Hagar happily discovered that Eddie had been working on a new idea in the same tempo, and with the same I/IV chord movement as 'Make it Last', matching his lyrics perfectly.

The track begins in a Montrose/Free style, with Hagar's bluesy moan over a crunching riff, although the heavy chorus on Eddie's guitar adds an eighties sheen. The great, stomping groove gives way to a melodic bridge, illuminated by beautifully poppy harmonies. The chorus manages the classic Van Halen trick of blending a catchy, singalong vocal line with rhythmically complex backing as Alex moves his kick and snare beats to unexpected positions in the bar, creating an appropriately unbalanced rhythm for a song inspired by a drunk's stagger. There's a superb solo, with Eddie playing long, arcing notes, developing into a passage of proggy arpeggios, cutting across the beat. After a return to the stripped-down dynamic of the intro and another bridge, an extended out-chorus fades on Eddie's chiming arpeggios. There's much to recommend the track: It's one of Hagar's more enjoyable lyrics, with a sense of fun that's less contrived than on the aforementioned 'Summer Nights'. The performances are superb, and the music strikes a fine balance between rock power and pop polish. My one criticism is that it's simply too long. At three or four minutes, 'Cabo Wabo' would be a perfect summer anthem, but it lacks sufficient substance to justify a bloated seven-minute run-time. Nevertheless, it's a joyful track, keeping Van Halen's party spirit alive, and for that reason, 'Cabo Wabo' remains a highlight of the 'Van Hagar' years.

'Source Of Infection' (Van Halen, Van Halen, Hagar, Anthony)

Reminiscing in *Red,* Sammy sums up this song thus: "Source of Infection', ugh'. So far, so promising! On a positive note, the instrumental track is terrific. After skipping *5150,* Van Halen's signature breakneck shuffle is back with a vengeance, picking back up where 'Hot for Teacher' left off. The intro sees Eddie's sequence of tapped arpeggios joined by Alex's racing double-bass shuffle. The verses are stripped-down, with jazzy syncopated runs and chords, while the bridge takes on a more serious minor-key tonality. The chorus riff is closely related to 'I'm the One' or the introduction of 'Hot for Teacher' – far from original, but a pleasing reminder of the band's classic sound. Beyond that, there are a couple of great solos – Eddie getting a lot of mileage out of worrying and gnawing at a single F note in the first, and the second having a much more wide-ranging construction. Alex is on top form too, swinging like crazy and dropping bop-like 'bombs', before winding the track up with a jazzy flourish. There were the makings of a minor classic in the instrumental track of 'Source of Infection', before Sammy got involved...

Conceived as a joke that only Sammy and Eddie found amusing, the 'lyrics' (I use the term loosely) consist of a stream of idiotic exclamations in place of verses ('Hey! Alright! How 'bout 'cha now, c'mon!') and choruses that continue 'Good Enough''s thread of grim sexist nonsense. Speaking to Popoff, Sammy acknowledged: 'It was very politically incorrect and personally, Eddie and I both kind of regret it'. An uncomfortable, embarrassing listen, then, and a waste of some solid musical ideas.

'Feels So Good' (Van Halen, Van Halen, Hagar, Anthony)

Thankfully, there's more to enjoy in 'Feels So Good', the album's third keyboard-based song. There's a hint of mid-eighties Genesis to it, although Alex's assured, swinging drums are a firm reminder of the band's heavier roots. Eschewing the glossy tones used on 'When it's Love', Eddie's keyboard here has a drier, early analogue synth-like sound, for a warmer feel. The main synth figure oscillates between the IV and V chords, while maintaining a low

C pedal point pulse. Eddie's rhythm guitar reinforces the pedal tone, sticking to a C power-chord while the keyboard harmonies move around it. The verse uses the well-worn I-VI-IV-V chord sequence, familiar from countless 1950s hits, with a bold poppy melody. The song modulates up a key for the bridge, with Anthony's high harmonies singing answering phrases to Hagar's lead. After the second bridge, the chorus arrives, based on the intro motif, with backing vocals echoing Sammy's lead with a yelled, 'So good!'.

The instrumental moves to an angsty minor key, with four bars of subdued keyboard preceding a strident guitar solo. Eddie strafes us with whinnying harmonic divebombs before building to a soaring climax. The final minute is all chorus, slowly fading as Hagar ad-libs. His lyrics are far from profound, their essential message being 'love is nice'. They also veer into clunky nonsense, with lines like 'Yesterday I was alone/ Suddenly I walked you home'. However, the song coheres in the bridge, with its 'I'll send a message in a bottle' refrain, which, although derivative of 'Message in a Bottle' (1979) by The Police, adds a pleasing image to illustrate our narrator's plight, which is elaborated in the second verse. Insubstantial lyrics aside, 'Feels So Good' is an excellent example of the 'mature', radio-friendly Van Halen sound – successfully blending 'Jump'-style synth-rock and Hagar's own soft rock stylings, packing enough punch to avoid descending into syrupy mush. Released as the fourth single from *OU812,* the song reached number 35 on the *Billboard* Hot 100, and stands up far better today than some of the band's more celebrated power ballads.

'Finish What Ya Started' (Van Halen, Van Halen, Hagar, Anthony)
The last track recorded for the album, this semi-acoustic slice of rootsy Americana, is unlike anything the band had done before or would do again. Nevertheless, it works remarkably well, with Eddie twanging out James Burton-esque clean-toned lead lines over a solid, Stones-y groove while Sammy strums a loose acoustic rhythm. It's a refreshing change for a band who had otherwise become less stylistically adventurous during the Hagar years, the laid-back style allowing Sammy to relax, showing a different side to his voice. It's also nice to hear the band back in a live-sounding setting, minus obvious eighties production gloss. A snappy, country-ish lick from Eddie brings in a loose, jammed intro, with Alex playing syncopated kick and snare, keeping time on the snare rim. The steady groove kicks in and doesn't let up until a stop-time instrumental, which features some convincing Merle Travis/ Chet Atkins-style picking from Eddie.

In *Red,* Sammy recalls Eddie appearing unannounced at his Malibu home in the early hours of the morning, interrupting an intimate conjugal moment, to insist that Sammy listen to a new idea: 'He started playing me the riff for 'Finish What Ya Started' and right away I got excited'. The chorus refrain Hagar wrote that night correctly predicted the frosty reception he'd receive upon returning to the bedroom after completing the song. However, although the theme of *coitus interruptus* is clearly implied, for once, Sammy is canny enough to couch it within a more general lyric about an unfulfilled relationship. It's still not exactly subtle, but 'Finish What Ya Started' is a fine rock n' roll song – slightly sleazy, without crossing the line into grossness. It struck a chord with the listening public, reaching number 13 on the Hot 100, when released as the album's third single in September 1988.

'Black And Blue' (Van Halen, Van Halen, Hagar, Anthony)

Outrageous bump n' grind rock is a Van Halen staple, so 'Black and Blue', a salacious stomp with gratuitous S&M lyrics, should be a sure-fire win. Unfortunately, instead of the tongue-in-cheek raunchiness of 'Beautiful Girls' or the gleeful darkness of 'Dirty Movies', 'Black and Blue' just sounds sad. Musically, it's a leaden plod, lacking the usual funk or swing. The main riff is generic, as though Eddie settled on the first thing his fingers landed on – unusual for such a restless innovator. There are a few impressive flourishes, including a woozy, echo-drenched guitar solo, and the band's distinctive harmonies do their best to brighten things up. Nevertheless, it remains one of the album's least inspiring tracks. Worst of all, Sammy's lyrics are among his most cringeworthy. The opening verse sets the tone: 'Slip n' slide, push it in/ Bitch sure got the rhythm'. Frankly, it's abysmal – vulgar, ugly and witless. We might forgive such cliched cock-rock drivel from a young, clueless band, fresh from Sunset Strip, but Van Halen were seasoned veterans by this point, with no excuse. Furthermore, it drags on, pushing past several obvious finishing points to a bloated five-and-a-half-minute running time.

The band themselves were pleased with the track, with Eddie describing it in *Eruption* as 'a great slippery grungy heavy funk song' and Sammy modestly describing it to Popoff as 'a masterpiece of phrasing'. However, in *Red,* his assessment of his lyrics is more circumspect, conceding that they were 'a little too eighties'. I'll say! Chosen as the album's lead single, it was released a month before the LP, and reached number 34 on the Hot 100. This wasn't a terrible showing but must have been a disappointment after the run of successful singles from *5150,* and one can't help but feel that there were plenty of better choices available.

'Sucker In A 3 Piece' (Van Halen, Van Halen, Hagar, Anthony)

There's a definite sense of 'filler' to this track, which shows promise but is sabotaged by a lack of imagination and taste. Opening with blaring overdriven chords from Eddie, it soon locks into an AC/DC-ish three-chord groove, not unlike 'Panama' or 'Everybody Wants Some!', but less catchy. The lyrics' premise – the narrator's girl being stolen by an older, balder, stouter but, crucially, wealthier rival – shows promise, and could have been fun in Roth's hands. However, with Hagar at the helm, the words come out sounding spiteful and dumb, peppered with grim misogyny. Hagar was unhappy that the 'politically correct' record company edited out his last sophomoric oral sex reference, but in truth, the track would have benefited from much more sweeping cuts. The main body of the song is monotonous, failing to develop from the initial riff, and lacking discernible hooks. In place of a melody, Sammy yowls around a couple of notes of the blues scale, with little to differentiate verse from chorus. Thankfully, things get slightly more interesting 3:22 in, with a new, four-chord pattern that builds ominously before exploding into a fierce, stinging guitar solo. Sadly, it's a short-lived reprieve, and we're soon back to the main riff for an unnecessary outro. Although there are promising moments, at nearly six minutes, the song's meagre ingredients are stretched very thin. Earlier Van Halen albums were tight 30-minute blasts, with half-baked ideas like 'Sucker in a 3 Piece' either being rejected or worked on and rewritten for future releases. Sadly, the CD era resulted in many artists creating longer, patchier albums, and Van Halen were no exception.

'A Apolitical Blues' (George) [CD-only bonus track]

This boozy, sloppy slow blues is a cover of a deep cut from Little Feat's 1972 sophomore LP, 'Sailin' Shoes', written by singer/guitarist Lowell George. The narrator bemoans his hard luck, as we'd expect in a blues number. However, the cause of his misery isn't any of the standard reasons (mean women, hard living, the devil ...), but his inability to relate to either side of the political spectrum, refusing to answer the phone to either communist dictator Chairman Mao, or notoriously right-wing actor John Wayne. It's an enjoyably sardonic comment on the tokenistic radicalism common in late-sixties/early-seventies popular culture. Little Feat's recording was produced by Ted Templeman with Donn Landee engineering. Accordingly, Landee was able to replicate their recording set-up, capturing the band live with a stereo pair of room mics. Eddie plays slide guitar on the left, with Sammy's electric rhythm on the right. The only overdub is a piano, added later by Eddie, who does a decent job of recreating Bill Payne's smoky juke-joint tinkling.

In the Roth era, Dave's cover choices were all about entertainment – potential hits that were danceable, diverting or amusing. By contrast, 'A Apolitical Blues' is more a statement of the band's authenticity, picking a wilfully obscure tune and trying to replicate the feel of the original. Compared to Little Feat's recording, there's a bleary looseness here, with the tempo dragging, some questionable tuning, and Eddie's slide frequently overshooting the intended note. It's an entertaining enough bonus track, but it's lucky the band came up with 'Finish What Ya Started' at the eleventh hour, as the LP would have been weaker with 'A Apolitical Blues' in the main track-list instead. As it is, the song is a downbeat conclusion to an album that has its share of lows but overall shows 'Van Hagar' cohering into a very solid band.

For Unlawful Carnal Knowledge (1991)

Personnel:
Sammy Hagar: lead vocals
Edward Van Halen: guitar, keyboards, electric drill on 'Poundcake', backing
vocals
Michael Anthony: bass, backing vocals
Alex Van Halen: drums, backing vocals
Additional personnel:
Steve Lukather: backing vocals on 'Top Of The World'
Recorded at 5150 Studios, March 1990 – April 1991
Produced by Ted Templeman, Andy Johns and Van Halen
Engineered by Lee Herschberg, Michael Scott and Andy Johns
Record label: Warner Brothers
Released June 17 June 1991
Highest chart position: US: 1 UK: 12
Running time: 52:00
Current edition: Rhino Records CD reissue

By the turn of the decade, the Hagar-fronted line-up was a well-established,
highly successful unit. Nevertheless, there were signs that their 'all-for-
one' camaraderie had started to ebb. Shortly after *OU812*, Eddie and Alex
proposed cutting Michael's financial stake in the band to a mere ten per
cent, effectively reducing him to a paid sideman. Hagar voted against the
motion, but Anthony – ever the appeaser – agreed. For the first time since
Roth left, the acrimony of old was resurfacing. Moreover, after several hectic
years, Hagar was keen to take time off to look after his wife, Betsy, whose
fragile mental health was worsened by Sammy's constant absence (not to
mention his compulsive, barely-concealed womanising). However, Eddie was
eager to escape his own rocky domestic reality through music. Eventually,
after a year out of action, the band returned to the studio, with Andy Johns
as producer, and without Landee for the first time. Johns, famed for his
engineering work on classic records by Led Zeppelin, The Rolling Stones
and many more, seemed a fine choice for an album the band envisioned as a
return to straight-ahead rock. Unfortunately, he was also a heavy drinker and,
with Alex now sober, quickly became Eddie's partner in crime. Consequently,
Eddie and Sammy had contrasting recollections of working with Johns: Eddie
found him an inspiring presence, who knew when to allow the band space
to develop an idea, although he also concedes in *Eruption* that 'he was an
alcoholic and you could only really get two hours out of him before things
would start going south'. In *Red,* Sammy is more cutting, calling Johns 'a
disaster', and recounting tales of crashed cars and erased takes. Eventually, at
Sammy's insistence, long-time producer and more recent *persona non grata*
Ted Templeman was brought in to finish recording the vocals and assist with
the mix.

The album took over a year to record, partly due to the difficulty of working with a perpetually inebriated producer and partly to Sammy's conscious effort to spend more time at home. Speaking to *Melodic Rock*, Sammy also admitted that the band were simply 'a little bit lazy', enjoying the spoils of success, rather than knuckling down to work. When finally completed in April 1991, the album was the band's longest to date, clocking in at a weighty 52 minutes, with two songs over the six-minute mark. As planned, it marked a clear sonic departure from the processed, very 'eighties' sound of their previous two albums. Eddie had built a drum room at 5150, finally making it possible to record a full acoustic kit there. The organic feel carried over to the album's keyboard songs, which were played on acoustic piano rather than synthesiser. This move towards a harder, less glossy sound was prescient in the early 1990s. The album was released just before the mainstream arrival of Nirvana, with the release of *Nevermind* in September 1991 and the subsequent explosion of grunge and alternative rock that all but wiped out the previous generation of heavy acts. Van Halen, sensing change in the air, took early evasive action. As the 1990s wore on, those of the band's arena rock peers who survived found themselves swapping spandex for street clothes, taming their teased-out hair, and cutting their own 'back-to-basics' records, such as Def Leppard's *Slang* (1996) and Motley Crue's eponymous 1994 effort.

The album's title was Hagar's idea. He originally wished to call the record 'Fuck censorship' as a none-too-subtle protest, inspired by the plight of 2 Live Crew – ironic, as Van Halen had sued the Florida rappers just the previous year for unauthorised use of a sample from 'Ain't Talkin' 'Bout Love' on 'The Fuck Shop' (1989). In the end, he settled for an acronym for the expletive, reducing his intended protest to sophomoric humour. In keeping with the stripped-down approach, the cover was simple and striking, featuring the band's iconic logo against a deep red leather background. Released in June 1991, the album gave the band their third consecutive US number one and reached number 12 in the UK. While fans eagerly welcomed the record, reviews were less kind, with most being middling and some quite damning; Gina Arnold in *Entertainment Weekly* cuttingly suggested that ''Dream another dream, this dream is over' may well be advice that Van Halen and their fans ought to take to heart'. Well, it's certainly not *that* bad! Like all the Hagar-era albums, it's bloated, includes some cringeworthy lyrics (although fewer this time), and has parts that feel overworked and under-inspired. For all that, it's the most consistent album of the Sammy years, with a welcome absence of drippy power ballads, and is sonically the best thing the band had made since *Diver Down.*

'Poundcake' (Van Halen, Van Halen, Hagar, Anthony)

The album opens with a sound effect produced by Eddie revving an electric drill over his guitar's pickup. Oddly, 'Poundcake' wasn't the first rock song of 1991 to make use of a drill, as Mr Big, ex-Dave Lee Roth bassist Billy Sheehan's hair metal combo, had released the dreadful 'Daddy, Brother, Lover, Little Boy (The Electric Drill Song)' just three months earlier. This featured both Sheehan and guitarist Paul Gilbert using drills with plectrum attachments to play hyper-speed tremolo lines. Thankfully, Eddie doesn't rely on gimmickry for long, and soon Alex's booming, Bonham-esque drums and Michael's full, warm bass bring the song to life. The guitars sound massive – a blend of overdriven six-string with a panned pair of cleaner 12-strings, creating a jangling wall of sound. Eddie had made some changes to his gear for this LP, altering his signature sound significantly. After years of customising and modifying guitars, he had moved into actual guitar design, creating a signature model with Ernie Ball/Musicman. Unlike his 'Frankenstrat', this featured two pickups, enabling more sonic possibilities. Furthermore, the Marshall 'Plexi' amplifier used on every previous LP was fading. Eddie was in the process of designing his own custom amp with Peavey but meanwhile used a Soldano amp on *For Unlawful Carnal Knowledge*, giving a subtly distinct tone. The riff of 'Poundcake' is merely a series of ringing chords over an open E pedal point – a common Van Halen trick. However, the blend of six and twelve-string sounds, unusual in hard rock, creates a distinctive, expansive effect. Jimmy Page used a similar blend on Led Zeppelin's 'The Song Remains the Same' (1973), so it's little surprise that the idea to use it here came from former Zeppelin collaborator Johns. The huge feel continues until the instrumental, where the sonic layers are stripped back, leaving just Eddie's lead and the rhythm section.

The trademark harmonies are notably absent, and with little melody, the song relies on Hagar's bluesy bellow, and the 'Uh ah uh ah ho' hook of the chorus. As Sammy's dodgy lyrics go, this ranks somewhere in the middle. It's ostensibly in praise of wholesome, natural womanhood, and there's welcome self-deprecation in the line 'It's getting hard to find/ Guess I ain't hip enough now'. However, Sammy's determination to use food metaphors to describe the female anatomy is toe-curling, veering dangerously close in tone to Warrant's risible cock-rock smash, 'Cherry Pie' (1990). Nevertheless, 'Poundcake' is an impactful album opener, and, aided by an expensive promo video, climbed to the top of the *Billboard* Mainstream Rock chart when released as the album's first single.

Judgement Day' (Van Halen, Van Halen, Hagar, Anthony)
The album steps up a gear with this chugging, metallic, but still hook-laden rocker. 'Judgement Day' finds Sammy railing against moralising Christians, telling them to 'get off my ass, get outta my face'. It's traditional rock n' roll anti-authoritarianism but misses an opportunity to do something more nuanced or satirical. Also, the second verse attempts some Roth-like wordplay but gets tangled up in repetitions of 'nothing' and 'anything', losing track of all meaning and rhyme scheme in the process. Still, the chorus hook of

'Put it off until judgement day/ I'll bear the cross on judgement day' neatly encapsulates the song's message and is catchy into the bargain.

The track starts with ringing arpeggios, bookended by a revving effect created by slackening the strings with the vibrato bar in a rapid 16th-note rhythm. This sets up the main riff, a palm-muted juggernaut in the tradition of Black Sabbath's 'Paranoid' (1970) or Led Zeppelin's 'Communication Breakdown' (1969). The verse proceeds in the same vein, with Sammy's forceful vocal matching the band's razor-sharp riffing. The bridge is the song's secret weapon – a brief burst of bright melody backed by glorious harmonies over a hopeful, ascending chord progression. Just as the tone seems on the verge of lightening, the chorus drags us back to lean, unrelenting riffage. After a second chorus, the instrumental begins with a bubbling sequence of two-handed dominant seventh arpeggios over a stop-time rhythm. Then, as the beat returns, there's a lead melody articulated with the whammy bar for an unsteady, lurching quality. A reprise of the intro is followed by an extended chorus, with Sammy executing a high two-tone scream not dissimilar to Dave's. Some more tapped arpeggios and a final shriek from Hagar wrap up this vigorous, well-structured rocker.

'Spanked' (Van Halen, Van Halen, Hagar, Anthony)

The album takes a quirky turn with this tongue-in-cheek heavy funk number. It opens with a long guitar note, played using an E-bow – an electronic device which creates forced string vibrations for violin-like sustain. The booming E minor riff is played on a Danelectro baritone guitar that Johns brought to the studio. Tuned an octave lower than a standard guitar, this allows Eddie to operate in the bass register alongside Mike. Alex plays a weighty groove with off-kilter accents, while Eddie overdubs choppy, clean chords reminiscent of Nile Rogers' playing for Chic. Over a more regular beat, the verse finds Sammy's narrator watching TV, and seeing a commercial that 'blew my mind'. The bridge moves to the relative major, sweetening the sound with harmonies before the jagged funk of the intro returns for the chorus. Here, the lyric reveals the nature of the 'mind-blowing' advert, with its slogan: 'Call her up on the spank line'. The subject of premium rate fetish chat lines seems like a ripe topic for a humorous, satirical lyric, which is presumably what Sammy is going for. Unfortunately, although 'Spanked' sets the scene well, the narrative doesn't go anywhere. Roth could tell a whole story in only a few lines. By contrast, over two sets of verses, bridges and choruses of 'Spanked', Hagar sets up a gag but doesn't deliver a punchline.

Nevertheless, there's still plenty to enjoy, not least the guitar solo, with the rhythm switching to a rocky stomp while Eddie breaks out his wah-wah pedal – a device he started using much more frequently around this time. This is followed by an atmospheric breakdown, with backing vocals treated with ghostly reversed reverb and eerie shrieks and howls from Eddie's guitar. The last chorus extends into a slow fade, with shards of wild echo-laden guitar and vocal ad-libs. It's an enjoyable listen, providing a glimpse of the band's sillier side, and broadening the album's sonic palette. However, it's not particularly substantial, and at nearly five minutes, would have benefitted from judicious editing.

'Runaround' (Van Halen, Van Halen, Hagar, Anthony)

We're back in driving rock territory with a song that finds the narrator chasing a girl who won't let him go but keeps him at arm's length. It's built on some great twangy riffing from Eddie, played on a Fender Telecaster for its trebly tone. This alternates with an enigmatic-sounding series of high arpeggios, creating an air of mystery, reflecting the elusive character of the song's subject. Van Halen's songs of this era are often constructed to a formula, and 'Runaround' is no exception: An introductory riff leads to a driving, bluesy verse. The bridge follows, brighter and more melodic, normally with added harmonies. Then it's back to hard-driving rock for the chorus, with backing vocals and bigger guitars added. Repeat, guitar solo, then a build to a final extended chorus. Structurally, it's predictable, but there's still much to savour. The bridge is one of their best, with an appealing, hopeful chord progression and soaring lead vocal, reflecting the narrator's quixotic optimism. There's even a lyrical nod to 'What a Fool Believes', the Doobie Brothers' 1979 hit, co-authored by erstwhile 'I'll Wait' collaborator Michael McDonald. The solo is a cracker, with Eddie once again using his wah pedal for extra colour, and the breakdown that follows finds Sammy singing in a low drawl, reminding us he can do more than just leather-lunged belting. The only slight let-down is the chorus, which is catchy but insubstantial, starting to grate with repetition. Again, some editing might have helped, but 'Runaround' remains a very decent rock song, albeit around a minute too long.

'Pleasuredome' (Van Halen, Van Halen, Hagar, Anthony)

All formulas are abandoned here as the band leap headlong into prog rock territory. Starting with a solo passage of gently picked arpeggios with twinkling harmonics, the serene mood is soon shattered by a thunderous tom fill. Alex's drum part for the introduction and verse is essentially one long, elaborate fill – a spectacular exercise in Keith Moon-style *sturm und drang*, with a vast cavernous sound. It's no surprise that in concert, this track was used as a springboard for Alex's solo spot. Mike holds the rhythm together with a solid 16th-note pedal point, over which Eddie lays tense, simmering chords and a double-tracked Sammy makes enigmatic spoken pronouncements. The bridge finally falls into a relatively regular beat, although Alex keeps things off-kilter, with every other snare beat landing a 16th note later than expected. Eddie strums sombre minor chords while Sammy swaps enigmatic speech for enigmatic singing. The chorus provides some pop gloss, with Sammy's lead climbing heroically while harmony backing vocals sing an answering phrase of 'miles and miles', their sugary tone at odds with the song's turbulent feel.

Musically, there's a strong hint of Rush, especially in the inexhaustible invention and muscularity of the drumming. The lyrics also seem inspired by Rush, their song 'Xanadu' (1977) in particular. The lyrics to this song are based on Samuel Taylor Coleridge's hallucinatory poem, *Kubla Kahn* (published in 1816), which begins with the lines: 'In Xanadu did Kubla Kahn/A stately pleasure dome decree'. Whereas Rush's song directly relates to Coleridge's poem, Hagar has simply borrowed the idea of a 'pleasure dome' and perhaps a hint of Xanadu's fantastical landscape, as his narrator goes 'tripping and stumbling through a land full of miracles'. Beyond that, Sammy's narrative is nebulous, with a vague otherworldliness that wouldn't withstand close scrutiny. In the past, Van Halen's secret weapon had been their ability to blend complex prog/fusion elements into concise, catchy pop formats. By contrast, there are numerous musically dazzling passages here but not much of a song to hold them together, and at nearly seven bombastic minutes, the effect is numbing.

'In 'n' Out' (Van Halen, Van Halen, Hagar, Anthony)

Another epic, clocking in at over six minutes. 'In 'n' Out' is essentially a blues song, using a slightly modified 12-bar format to accompany Hagar's screed on the endless cycle of debt that dominates many lives. As Sammy tells it, however hard you work and however much you earn, the system leaves you back where you started: 'They got you goin' in, they got you comin' out/ Same amount, in 'n' out'. This is a relatable sentiment, describing the day-to-day experience of many regular people. Nevertheless, there's something unappealing about hearing such complaints from a multi-millionaire rock star who hasn't known hardship for decades! The track is solid hard rock, with rich, layered guitar textures, blending a melodic main riff with choppy power-chord rhythm and searing lead. The verses are divided in two, with the first half in stop-time while a heavy funk beat powers the second half along. In the chorus, Eddie replaces the V chord of a standard 12-bar progression with jazzy sus7/9 chords, adding much-needed flavour to this 'meat and potatoes' blues-rock number.

Eddie's solo is appropriately blues-based, once again using wah-wah. It starts as a back-and-forth with Sammy, introducing the motif that later becomes the out-chorus hook, and continues for a second 12-bar stretch, adding some wild *Pac Man* sound effect-style divebombs and fierce shredding. Another verse and chorus lead to a sudden halt as Sammy sings, 'Goin' out!'. This would have been a perfect point to end the track, but instead, there's another two minutes of 'Uh uh uh yeah, in 'n' out', which quickly wears thin. While 'In 'n' Out' isn't a bad song, there's nothing outstanding about it either, and for all the band's efforts, it ultimately feels overlong and overdone.

'Man on a Mission' (Van Halen, Van Halen, Hagar, Anthony)

The album's mid-order slump continues with 'Man on a Mission' which, frustratingly, features some top-notch musical ideas shackled to a thoroughly middling song. It starts promisingly with a quirky bebop-like introduction featuring a dissonant high melody over a chromatically descending walking bass. The swinging rhythm carries over to the main riff, which dances nimbly up the fretboard, decorated with pinch harmonics and bluesy filigree. Alex's drums are simple and powerful, with a strong underlying swing. Unfortunately, after this fine beginning, the song is a letdown. The lyrics are bog-standard macho nonsense, our narrator bragging about how he's going to get the girl, and what he's going to do to her when he does. Hagar strains at the top of his register throughout, which quickly becomes wearing. Even the backing vocals – normally a highlight – are a bit 'off' here, sung in a weird mock-seductive coo, possibly intended to be humorous, but actually just creepy-sounding. The guitar solo, inevitably, is blazing, with Alex deconstructing the beat beneath Eddie's feet as he plays, and the slashing power chords of the middle eight provide a change of timbre. Mostly, though, 'Man on a Mission' stays on one level, with little variation. Being charitable, we could assume this deliberately reflects the narrator's unwavering determination, but even so, it doesn't make for a tremendously interesting listen.

'The Dream is Over' (Van Halen, Van Halen, Hagar, Anthony)

The economic cynicism of 'In 'n' Out' resurfaces in this bitter song, which captures the sense of betrayal many Americans felt as the eighties bubble burst and recession loomed in the early 1990s. The 'dream' referred to is the American dream itself – the idea that, with honest hard work and dedication, anyone can make their fortune. Millions grow up believing this ideal, but Sammy tells us, 'It's a rip-off, we're stepped on and cheated'. It's a bleak outlook; the song tells us to 'Dream another dream, this dream is over', but as an alternative, provides only dark hints that a less-honest approach might be 'your ticket out of poverty'. As with 'In 'n' Out', a disconnect occurs when a multi-millionaire megastar lectures us about the plight of the common man, but to Hagar's credit, 'The Dream is Over' is a much more compelling and effective lyric. The music is punchier and more interesting than the two preceding tracks too. Introduced by Hagar's whisper of 'C'mon man, wake up!', it moves swiftly from a thumping stop-time introduction to a soaring guitar melody. This was played with a slide in the studio, although in live performances, Eddie simulated the slide effect with skilful string bends. Eddie's rhythm playing is terrific, shaping the song's dynamics as he moves smoothly between stabbing staccato chords, fluid Andy Summers-style muted arpeggios and sinuous octave melodies that snake around the vocal line. Unusually, the chorus doesn't appear until halfway through, but it's worth the wait – instantly memorable, with angelic harmonies and a Byrds-like chiming

12-string guitar. There's an explosive solo over a reprise of the intro, a re-run of the slide section, and a breakdown bridge. After that, the final minute is devoted to the chorus, extended over a slow fade. Van Halen may have started out as a party band, but 'The Dream is Over' reflects a much more cynical and perhaps more grown-up outlook. As 'mature' Van Halen songs go, it's a good one – well-arranged, impactful and concise, with a musically uplifting chorus that offsets the lyrics' bleakness.

'Right Now' (Van Halen, Van Halen, Hagar, Anthony)

Considered by Sammy to be among his finest work with the band, 'Right Now' is another song with aspirations of maturity. The music dates back to at least 1984. After it had been vetoed by Roth, Eddie used an instrumental version of the track in the score he composed for *The Wild Life* (Art Linson, 1984). When recording *For Unlawful Carnal Knowledge*, Sammy heard him playing the keyboard piece and realised it fit perfectly with the lyrics he was writing. Eddie's atmospheric piano intro is soon joined by a pounding rhythm section, with Mike on particularly fine form. As the song slips into gear, the piano plays the main chordal riff, with guitar and rhythm section providing a bombastic counterpoint. The strident minor key verse gives way to a brighter bridge, with Eddie adding a touch of organ to the mix. The chorus banishes the last of the verse's brooding tone with a joyous gospel-inflected feel, making great use of harmonies. Throw in the usual superb guitar solo, and you have a well-constructed, effective pop-rock song.

That said, I find it perplexing that the song carries such special importance for so many, the band included. In *Red*, Hagar describes it as 'the first serious lyric I had written for Van Halen, a big statement', and clearly considers it a watershed moment in his career. The early 1990s were a momentous time on the world stage, with the fall of the Iron Curtain suggesting the possibility of a new era of enlightened peace. Sammy may have intended for 'Right Now' to capture the spirit of the age, but the lyrics actually amount to little more than a string of trite motivational slogans: 'Right now, it's your tomorrow', 'Catch that magic moment' etc. While some of Hagar's lyrics ('Mine All Mine', for example) do grapple with serious issues, 'Right Now' merely provides vague platitudes about seizing the moment and making a positive change. It's very much in the mould of songs written to accompany training montages in 1980s sports movies, such as Joe Esposito's 'You're the Best' (1984) or Survivor's 'Eye of the Tiger' (1982). The music fits this template too – keyboard-driven soft-rock, moving from moody minor key verses to a triumphant major-key chorus, all at a steady-yet-determined mid-tempo pace. Eddie compared the gospel-tinged chorus to Joe Cocker's 'Feelin' Alright' (1968), but it's closer to Michael Jackson's 'Man in the Mirror' (1988), with which it shares a I, III, IV, V chord progression and similar lyrical sentiment. Obviously, 'Right Now' isn't my cup of tea, but it resonates with millions of fans across the world, aided by the fact that the vague lyrics allow each listener to imprint it with their own personal meaning. Certainly, video director Mark Fenske treated the song as a blank canvas in the promo clip, which featured a series of slogans covering a range of topics, all beginning with the words 'right now'. The single wasn't a massive success, peaking at number 55 on the Hot 100, but the video won 'Video of the Year' at the 1992 MTV Video Music Awards, helping to cement the song's place as one of the milestones of the Hagar era.

'316' (Van Halen, Van Halen, Hagar, Anthony)
Eddie hadn't recorded a solo guitar piece for a Van Halen record since *Diver Down*, so '316' was a timely inclusion on the album. However, anyone expecting 'Eruption'-style pyrotechnics would have been disappointed by this gentle acoustic interlude. Although the piece dated back to at least 1986, having appeared in Eddie's solo segments on the *5150* tour, it had recently been pressed into service as a lullaby for his new-born child, Wolfgang, and its title reflects Wolf's birth date: 16 March 1991. The track is played on a Gibson Chet Atkins solid-body acoustic, processed through an Eventide Harmonizer – a device Eddie used to create artificial doubling effects on his electric tones from the mid-eighties onwards. It's one of the simplest pieces he ever composed – a pretty, chordal melody with a hint of blues around the edges, picked softy and played with minimal ornamentation, aside from a little flurry of tapped harmonics at the very end.

'Top of the World' (Van Halen, Van Halen, Hagar, Anthony)
The album closes with, for my money, the finest pop song of the Hagar era. It resurrects the guitar line from the fade-out of 'Jump', transposes it into E major, and uses it as the basis for a joyful, uncomplicated classic. Curiously, Eddie wasn't keen on the song, saying in *Eruption* that 'we had five other tunes that I would've preferred to use that didn't make it on the album'. Nevertheless, Johns insisted on its inclusion, and rightly so! Although the signature riff was already familiar from 'Jump', it had previously appeared in live renditions of 'Dance the Night Away', and it's that song that 'Top of the World' most closely resembles. Like the aforementioned classic, 'Top of the World' has a relentlessly upbeat tone and a similar three-chord structure. The chorus, in particular, is a close relative of the 1979 hit, with its dazzling harmonies (bolstered by a guest appearance from Toto's Steve Lukather) and Eddie's tapped harmonic counter-melody. The only hint of darkness comes in the first eight bars of the instrumental. Here, we shift to an E minor as searing wah-wah guitar and thunderous tom fills cut through the sunshine. The clouds soon part, however, finding Eddie back in a major key, harmonising with himself across two tracks. There's a brief return to the intro riff, and then the chorus extends to a fade. Thankfully, Sammy recognised that a lighter touch was required for the lyrics of 'Top of the World', putting the self-conscious 'maturity' evident elsewhere on the album

aside in favour of infectious optimism. It's lightweight, but for once, that's the point, and despite Eddie's reservations, 'Top of the World' became the only single from the album to crack the top forty of the Hot 100, reaching number 27.

Live: Right Here, Right Now (1993)

Personnel:
Sammy Hagar: lead vocals
Edward Van Halen: guitar, keyboards, backing vocals
Michael Anthony: bass, backing vocals
Alex Van Halen: drums
Additional personnel:
Alan Fitzgerald: keyboards, backing vocals
Recorded at Selland Arena, Fresno, California, 14-15 May, 1992
Produced by Andy Johns and Van Halen
Engineered by Biff Dawes
Record label: Warner Brothers
Release date: 26 January 1993
Highest chart position: US: 5, UK: 24
Running time: 141:29
Current edition: Rhino Records CD reissue
Tracklisting: 'Poundcake', 'Judgement Day', 'When it's Love', 'Spanked', 'Ain't
Talkin' 'Bout Love', 'In 'n' Out', 'Dreams', 'Man on a Mission', 'Ultra Bass', 'Pleasure
Dome/Drum Solo', 'Panama', 'Love Walks In', 'Runaround', 'Right Now', 'One Way
to Rock', 'Why Can't This be Love', 'Give to Live', 'Finish What Ya Started', 'Best
of Both Worlds', '316', 'You Really Got Me/Cabo Wabo', 'Won't Get Fooled Again',
'Jump', 'Top of the World'
Bonus disc (German and Japanese editions only): 'Eagles Fly', 'Mine All Mine'

Live albums have long been a popular way for bands to fill a gap between
studio records, generate extra income, and provide a permanent document of
their live show for fans, so it's surprising that Van Halen – a formidable live
act – waited so long to release their own. In their prolific early years, there
was no need for a schedule filler. However, as their work rate relaxed in the
1990s, a live record seemed a viable way to keep the band in the public eye
while they took a much-needed rest.

They recorded and filmed a couple of shows in Fresno, towards the end of
the *For Unlawful Carnal Knowledge* tour, and a double CD-length track list
was compiled from the tapes. While Sammy escaped to Maui with his new
partner, the brothers began mixing the record. This seemed a simple task
until they started to make a few minor studio tweaks, fixing the occasional
fluffed note, misplaced beat or out-of-tune passage. This snowballed until,
according to Hagar in *Red,* they had effectively re-recorded the entire
album's music:

> They fixed everything. Only now that Eddie was playing in tune, my
> singing's off-key. And where Al sped up in 'Runaround', now I'm singing
> ahead of the beat. Now I had to go back in the studio and redo all my
> vocals. I wanted to kill those guys.

A furious Hagar returned from Hawaii to sing the entire concert again. It's not clear whether Mike was also summoned to rerecord the bass, but given the lack of respect the band afforded him by this point, it's possible that Eddie simply re-recorded his parts.

Live albums are often tidied up or enhanced a little in post-production. However, *Live: Right Here, Right Now* sounds *very* slick, retaining little of the spontaneity and excitement of a live performance. It's also *very* long, filling two entire CDs to capacity. Despite this epic run-time, there are still only four Roth-era songs, while all of the most recent album is recreated, except for 'The Dream is Over', which crops up on the DVD version. There are also lengthy solo spots from each instrumentalist, two songs from Hagar's solo catalogue and a cover of a classic by The Who. The album reached number 5 on the US album chart, but it wasn't the live document fans had craved, and the fraught circumstances of its production soured relationships within the band. Although most songs are familiar from their studio versions, there were a few titles which had not appeared on previous Van Halen records, detailed below:

'Ultra Bass' (Van Halen, Van Halen, Hagar, Anthony)
Michael Anthony is a fine, often underrated bassist, but do we need to hear him playing a five-minute solo? Not really. He does his best to generate interest, starting with broken chords played with a timed delay, then engaging his Micro Synth for some space-age sounds. Alex joins in as Mike segues into a bit of 'Sunday Afternoon in the Park', which then descends into several minutes of clanging distorted noise and feedback. It's one thing to witness this at a show, with Mike wigging out on his custom Jack Daniels bottle-shaped bass, but on CD, it's tempting to lunge for the 'skip' button.

'One Way to Rock' (Hagar)
Originally featured on Sammy's 1982 LP, *Standing Hampton,* 'One Way to Rock' is as basic and block-headed as the title suggests. It teeters on the brink of *Spinal Tap*-style parody, reaching a nadir with the line 'Crank up the drums, Mikey's bass, and my Les Paul in your face!'. Still, it's a fun, lively performance, with Hagar playing second guitar (in the right channel) and trading solos with Eddie, culminating in a corny dual harmony lead.

'Give to Live' (Hagar)
If 'One Way to Rock' was silly but enjoyable, 'Give to Live', drawn from Sammy's 1987 opus, *I Never Said Goodbye* is sadly neither. Originally a bombastic power ballad, the song is given the painfully-earnest acoustic treatment here. It's nearly six minutes of a solo Hagar strumming artlessly and emoting screechily, and while Sammy fans might enjoy this, it doesn't belong on a Van Halen record. Next!

'Won't Get Fooled Again' (Townshend)

The band sound like they're having a fine time on this cover of The Who's 1971 anthem. Eddie does a decent job of replicating Pete Townshend's VCS synth-treated organ on his guitar for the intro, and elsewhere recreates Pete's lead lines faithfully while throwing in some Van Halen-isms for good measure. Alex keeps more of a regular pulse than Keith Moon was wont to, but still throws in plenty of the unexpected tom flurries and explosive fills that made Moon so influential. Hagar's leathery rasp is well suited to the song too, and the whole thing comes off well. Not essential listening but a spirited, enjoyable encore.

'Eagles Fly' (Hagar)

This was released as an extra track on the CD single of the live version of 'Jump', and also surfaced on a bonus disc included with German and Japanese editions of the album. It's another Sammy acoustic solo number taken from *I Never Said Goodbye*. Again, it's over five minutes of achingly dull power balladry with lyrics that desperately want to sound meaningful but remain nonsensical. With apologies to any Sammy die-hards, this has no place anywhere near a Van Halen record.

Balance (1995)

Personnel:
Sammy Hagar: lead vocals
Edward Van Halen: guitar, keyboards, backing vocals
Michael Anthony: bass, backing vocals
Alex Van Halen: drums
Additional personnel:
Steve Lukather: backing vocals on 'Not Enough'
The Monks of Gyuto Tantric University: chants on 'The Seventh Seal'
Recorded at 5150 Studios, Little Mountain Sound Studios, May – September 1994
Produced by Bruce Fairbairn
Engineered by Erwin Musper and Mike Plotnikoff
Record label: Warner Brothers
Release date: 24 January 1995
Highest chart position: US: 1, UK: 8
Running time: 53:18
Current edition: Rhino Records CD reissue

By the time Van Halen reconvened for *Balance*, there was significant animosity within the band. Sammy's long-time manager, Ed Leffler, who had also taken on Van Halen when Hagar joined the band, had sadly passed away in 1993. His replacement, Alex's brother-in-law Ray Danniels, was the Van Halen brothers' choice, with Sammy strongly opposed to his appointment. Tensions were exacerbated by Eddie's mental and physical state. He was in agony from a necrotic hip and in need of surgery. Simultaneously, he was attempting to quit the heavy drinking that had been a constant throughout his adult life. This combination of circumstances made him especially volatile and difficult to work with. Whether Eddie was sober for most of the recording, as he claimed, or secretly drinking throughout, as Hagar maintained, he became an increasingly vocal critic of Hagar's work. The tension eventually became so unbearable that Sammy and producer Bruce Fairbairn relocated to Vancouver to record the last five lead vocal tracks. While recording *For Unlawful Carnal Knowledge* had been a relaxed, drawn-out process, *Balance* was made over a much shorter time period, with the band putting in long shifts, grinding out the record through the hostility and infighting.

Both Sammy and Eddie credited Fairbairn with keeping the recording process on track. A veteran used to coaxing massive egos into producing successful albums (Aerosmith and Bon Jovi were among his multi-platinum clients), Fairbairn was a sensible choice. Even on the verge of collapse, the band managed to create a solid set of songs. The joy and camaraderie of yore were gone, but there was still plenty to please fans of previous Van Hagar offerings. The sleeve featured an image of squabbling conjoined twins, sitting on one end of a see-saw in a bleak, post-apocalyptic landscape – an on-the-nose symbol of the fractious state of the band, and of Sammy and Eddie's

relationship in particular. Released in January 1995, it gave the band their
fourth consecutive US number one and reached number eight in the UK,
too, comfortably outselling its predecessor. Dutifully, the band embarked on
an accompanying tour, soon dubbed the 'Ambulance' tour, due to Eddie's
increasingly severe hip issues, and Alex's ruptured vertebra, which required
him to play in a neck brace. A European leg didn't help the band's mood,
as they suffered the ignominy of supporting soft-rock behemoths, Bon
Jovi, whose fanbase were indifferent to Van Halen. The tour ended with
Eddie drinking openly and barely on speaking terms with Hagar. Although
Sammy would record one more song with the band ('Humans Being', for the
soundtrack to *Twister* (1996, Jan de Bont)), a plan to bring back Roth and
have both singers record new songs for a greatest hits album was the final
straw, and by June 1996, Van Hagar was no more.

'The Seventh Seal' (Van Halen, Van Halen, Hagar, Anthony)
The opening track of *Balance* is a bold statement, bleak and uncompromising,
with questing, oblique lyrics, far removed from the 'party rock' that Eddie
was keen to leave behind. In the wake of grunge, with its emphasis on raw
introspection, more abrasive sounds and punk-inspired anti-rock-star aesthetic,
the extrovert eighties rock archetype seemed painfully dated. Accordingly,
'The Seventh Seal' sounds nothing like 1980s hair metal, and not much like
Van Halen either. Opening, rather pretentiously, with chanting Tibetan monks,
the track soon hits a strident mid-tempo pace. The hammering drums and
full-toned 16th note bass throb have a familiar rock feel, but the guitar part
is a departure. Using heavy delay and reverb, Eddie plays a series of simple
two-note chords, creating a huge, echoing wall of sound, reminiscent of
U2's The Edge. Lead breaks are brief and understated, and aside from the
return of Eddie's flanger pedal, not heard since the Roth days, there are few
recognisable Van Halen characteristics. Sammy's lyrics are steeped in religious
imagery and references to the films of Swedish auteur Ingmar Bergman. The
title refers to Bergman's 1957 film of the same name, which in turn, takes its
title from a line in *Revelations*, pertaining to God's silence in response to the
deeds of sinners and the pleas of the innocent. We're a long way from 'Cabo
Wabo' here! The lyric doesn't directly relate to this film (or to 'The Virgin
Spring', a 1960 Bergman movie which is also referenced). However, both song
and film are, broadly speaking, depictions of a spiritual journey, with Hagar
using the imagery of baptism to invoke a plea for renewal. This nebulous
theme is lent authority by a barnstorming performance from Hagar, singing
with an intensity to rival the likes of Soundgarden's Chris Cornell. 'The Seventh
Seal', then, is an ambitious and impactful opener, but not much fun.

'Can't Stop Lovin' You' (Van Halen, Van Halen, Hagar, Anthony)
After an uncompromising start, the album takes an accessible turn with
this ready-made radio hit, written to order when Fairburn suggested the

album needed a poppier single. It's based on the timeless I, VI, IV, V chord progression with a chorus that uses just the first three notes of a major scale – a combination used in songs like 'Goodnite, Sweetheart, Goodnite' (1954) by The Spaniels and thousands of others since. The track's semi-acoustic soft-rock jangle strongly resembles Del Amitri's 1992 US top 40 hit, 'Always the Last to Know', with which it shares a key, tempo and portions of melody. There's nothing jarring or challenging to the track, from Eddie's sweet-toned tasteful leads to the angelic backing vocals and Sammy's heartfelt huskiness – it's all calculated top 40 fodder. However, the song is more than a mere exercise in cynical commerciality. Sammy's lyrics draw on the experience of his recent painful divorce, being written from the perspective of his ex-wife, imagining her feelings at leaving behind a 26-year relationship and watching her ex-partner move on. That said, Hagar is too commercially savvy to make the song overly specific, keeping his lyrics couched in broad, relatable terms. He also throws in a nod to Ray Charles' 1962 soul/country crossover hit, 'I Can't Stop Loving You', a version of Don Gibson's 1957 song, with a lyric that expresses similar sentiments to Hagar's. Listeners hungering for the rowdy sound of early Van Halen would be disappointed, but the song became a firm favourite of fans who came to the band via their later radio hits. Released as the album's second single, it reached number 30 on the Hot 100 and number 33 in the UK, becoming the band's last top 40 hit in either country

'Don't Tell Me (What Love Can Do)' (Van Halen, Van Halen, Hagar, Anthony)

This song, written as Sammy's response to the death of Kurt Cobain, was a bone of contention between the singer and Eddie. Hagar wanted the song to have a positive message, finding an uplifting lesson in the tragedy of Cobain's suicide, but claims that Eddie dismissed this concept as 'wimpy'. In *Red,* he recalls:

> I wanted it to say, 'I want to show you what love can do.' Ed and Al fought me on that. They wanted more of a grungy, bad-attitude song. 'Don't tell me what love can do.' That's not what I had in mind. I was talking about somebody who could have saved Kurt Cobain's life.

While we'll never know how the track would have sounded had Hagar got his way, the revised lyrics are a good match for Eddie's bleak, unforgiving music. It's a relentless minor-key dirge, with a plodding tempo and an unusually harsh, trebly guitar tone. The chorus offers a brief respite, with a burst of major-key melody and some welcome harmonies, but soon returns us to the grim, trudging verse. Even Eddie's solo feels despairing rather than triumphant. It's beautifully played, but with the tempo dropping to an even more ponderous half-time feel and his sound drowned in cavernous echo, there's a striking sense of emptiness and desolation to it. It's not a bad record by any means. Hagar gives a fine performance, singing with utter conviction, and the track has a stark, compelling power. Still, it's undeniably joyless – once an unthinkable accusation to level at a Van Halen record.

'Amsterdam' (Van Halen, Van Halen, Hagar, Anthony)

Another song that broadened the rift between singer and guitarist, 'Amsterdam' takes a powerhouse hard-rock backdrop and marries it to Sammy's clumsily captured impressions of the Van Halen brothers' birthplace. Always fond of a cliche, Hagar's take on the historic city focuses on pot smoking, the red-light district and little else. The chorus ('Wham bam Amsterdam, yeah, yeah, yeah/ Stone you like nothin' else can') has a cheesy eighties hair-metal feel, totally at odds with the more serious direction Eddie envisioned for the band and frankly rather embarrassing. It's a shame, as the track is musically strong, a Zeppelin-esque hip-swinging swagger, blending classic rock with a contemporary fuzzed-out down-tuned weightiness.

The instrumental has a classic Van Halen feel, beginning with a tension-building unison guitar and bass riff, before letting go with an entertainingly unpredictable queasy, careering solo. It's a riff-heavy monster of a track, and if you ignore the lyrics, sounds like a relative of 'Drop Dead Legs'. Despite Eddie's reservations, the song was released as the album's fourth single and was promptly banned by MTV for its drug-referencing lyrics, which did nothing to ease the guitarist's resentment. In retrospect, 'Amsterdam' is the sound of Hagar trying to keep the party alive, but unfortunately, Eddie was no longer in a partying mood.

'Big Fat Money' (Van Halen, Van Halen, Hagar, Anthony)

Putting aside down-tuned sludginess and grungy angst, 'Big Fat Money' is a straight-ahead rock n' roll barnstormer. Based on a modified 12-bar blues, its hectic energy is compounded by Hagar's mile-a-minute syllable-laden vocal line, recalling both Chuck Berry's oft-imitated 'Too Much Monkey Business' (1956) and the band's own 'Top Jimmy'. Elsewhere on *Balance*, Eddie deliberately avoids his sonic trademarks, exploring more contemporary sounds. Here, he simply lets rip with some classic 'brown sound' riffs and leads, as well as a wild, jazzy solo. The cleaner tone and slap-back echo used on this section were suggested by Fairbairn when Eddie was struggling to find the right approach. Played on a semi-acoustic Gibson ES-335, the solo is a whimsical bop-inflected joy, a reminder of the 'anything goes' spirit of the early years. This fun, feisty track is only let down by Sammy's avaricious lyrics. Such glorification of wealth wouldn't have raised an eyebrow in the 'greed is good' 1980s. However, by the nineties, the punk-influenced anti-materialistic ethic of Nirvana and their grunge brethren made such money-grubbing seem crass. It's a shame, as otherwise, the track is a welcome reminder of the excitement of old.

'Strung Out' (Van Halen, Van Halen, Hagar, Anthony)

This curious interlude was recorded over a decade earlier than the rest of *Balance*. Bruce Fairburn asked Eddie to come up with an instrumental introduction to 'Not Enough', prompting the guitarist to recall a tape dating back to his stay in a Malibu beach house rented from Broadway and Hollywood composer Marvin Hamlisch. The house contained a beautiful grand piano, which a less-than-sober Eddie decided to use for some avant-garde musical experimentation. As he explains in Eruption:

> I went in the kitchen and grabbed forks and knives and started scraping the strings on the inside of the piano to create all these different sounds. In the process, I wasted his fuckin' piano.

He goes on to liken the piece to a 'terrible B-level horror soundtrack', which is a fair assessment. It's atmospheric enough, but do we really need the full 1.29 of Eddie attacking a piano with the contents of a cutlery drawer?

'Not Enough' (Van Halen, Van Halen, Hagar, Anthony)

The opening piano chords and synth strings of 'Not Enough' suggest we might be in for another 'Love Walks In'- style power-ballad. Thankfully, the ensuing song is a more sombre, subtle affair. It still packs some rock punch in its choruses but avoids the pitfall of empty bombast. Instead, the song's reserved power, rich harmonies (aided again by Toto's Steve Lukather) and hymn-like verses are genuinely moving. The lyrics draw on the emotional hardships of Hagar's recent divorce and benefit from their simplicity. Sometimes, Sammy's words become mired in cliches and mixed metaphors. Here, he expresses universal sentiments in clear, unaffected language, and it's so much more effective. His delivery conveys real feeling too, without straining or over-singing. Anthony adds a lush, swooping, fretless bassline, recalling the iconic session work of Pino Palladino on Paul Young and Don Henley's solo records. Meanwhile, Eddie's solo soars majestically, using a Leslie rotating speaker effect like George Harrison did on The Beatles' similarly hymn-like 'Let it Be' (1970). I'm no fan of most Hagar-era ballads, but 'Not Enough' is a superior creation – heartfelt rather than cloying, dignified rather than overblown. As a single, it fared far worse than the band's previous ballads, just scraping into the Hot 100 at number 97. Nevertheless, it's a fine piece of work and should be remembered among the Hagar era's highlights.

'Aftershock' (Van Halen, Van Halen, Hagar, Anthony)

If 'Not Enough' dealt with the fallout from Sammy's divorce with pathos and empathy, 'Aftershock' does the opposite, taking a tough, defiant tone. It's essentially an aggrieved post-break-up diatribe, complaining of the hardship of 'living in the aftershock' of the relationship, and, unfortunately, lacks any recognisable hook. There's little melody, and the arrangement is overly-busy, suggesting the band tried to compensate for the absence of one really good idea by throwing together lots of half-baked ones. From the opening guitar motif that's a little too close to the riff of Metallica's 1991 mega-hit 'Enter Sandman', to the verse's bassline, which is straight out of Johnny Kidd & the Pirates' "Shakin' All Over" (1960), it's clear that original ideas are in short supply. There's impressively athletic playing from both brothers, strong backing vocals from Mike, and the mellow, melodic middle eight provides some variety, although it feels like it's been dropped in from a completely different song. Ultimately, for all the effort the band clearly expended, the end result is neither memorable nor enjoyable. It's the sound of a great band treading water for five-and-a-half minutes, and the album would be leaner and stronger without it.

'Doin' Time' (Van Halen, Van Halen, Hagar, Anthony)

The album's second instrumental is a rare solo showcase for Alex. It begins with a percussion loop, over which he builds a web of increasingly complex rhythmic patterns. At the 56-second mark, there's a sudden tempo change, and the track erupts into a full-blown drum solo. A cowbell keeps time as Alex plays rapid-fire triplet phrases around his sizeable kit. He eventually settles into a heavy, pounding tribal rhythm before bringing the track to a sudden conclusion with a terse cymbal grab. I'm a big fan of Alex's playing, and 'Doin' Time' would excite a concert audience. As an album track, however, it's hardly essential and likely to have listeners reaching for the 'skip' button.

'Baluchitherium' (Van Halen, Van Halen, Hagar, Anthony)

Yet another instrumental, 'Baluchiterium' is considerably more fully realised than either 'Strung Out' or 'Doin' Time'. It finds Eddie dipping his toe into the virtuoso instrumental rock popularised by Joe Satriani and Steve Vai, the leading lights of the post-Van Halen school of technically gifted shredders. The track is built on a thumping Bonham-like drumbeat and monstrous bass riff, played by Michael, and doubled by Eddie on a six-string bass for extra impact. The title, suggested by Eddie's wife, refers to a species of giant pre-historic land mammal, whose crunching footsteps are evoked by the pummelling groove. The track alternates between pared-down, riff-based sections and a bold melodic passage with a fuller, more heavily overdubbed sound. Three minutes in, everything breaks down to a programmed rhythm pattern as Eddie creates a jungle ambience, conjuring an assortment of animal sounds from his guitar. His dog, Sherman, also makes a cameo, which was captured by taping a hot dog to a microphone! Your enjoyment of 'Baluchitherium' will depend on your tolerance for slick muso rock, aimed more at other musicians than general listeners. Personally, I find it tedious. Eddie was an untouchable player, but there are better ways in which to appreciate his talent than listening to this four-and-a-half minutes of filler.

'Take Me Back (Déjà vu)' (Van Halen, Van Halen, Hagar, Anthony)

This bitter-sweet look back at a lost love strives for the catchy soft-rock sound of the Hagar-era band's biggest hits. The ingredients seem solid enough: breezy acoustic jangling on the verses, a soaring chorus with added power-chord crunch, and a wistful, slightly Beatles-ish middle eight. However, the lack of inspiration that dogged 'Aftershock' is in evidence here too, with several key elements sounding eerily familiar. The intro, with its softly-strummed descending chords over a ringing open D string, is strikingly similar to Bad Company's archetypical power-ballad 'Feel Like Makin' Love' (1974), and the acoustic riff that follows is a close relative of the main guitar motif of Led Zeppelin's 'Over the Hills and Far Away' (1973). There's nothing that could be considered plagiarism, but the influences are too transparent, especially as the finished product is a pale shadow of the songs from which it draws. Some of Sammy's lyrics on *Balance* are surprisingly potent, but 'Take Me Back' is about as lightweight as it gets: he sees someone who looks vaguely familiar and is reminded of a past love, and an idyllic holiday on 'some desert island off Morocco'. And that's all. While Van Halen's early work was characterised by its unfettered spontaneity, this feels like the adequate product of competent professionals, working with grim efficiency but no discernible joy or spark.

'Feelin'' (Van Halen, Van Halen, Hagar, Anthony)

Most editions of *Balance* close with this brooding epic, consisting of over six tempestuous minutes of minor-key introspection. It includes rare lyrical input from Eddie, who says in *Eruption*:

> The was a song on *Balance* called 'Feelin'' and one of the best lines in the song was, 'If I were you and you were me, which one would you rather be'…and that was something I wrote.

It's not clear if Eddie made any further contribution to the lyrics. They're somewhat inarticulate and disordered but convey confusion and disillusionment about many aspects of life, including personal image ('Grow it long, shave it off' – perhaps referring to Eddie's recent decision to crop his trademark flowing locks); the need to stay relevant ('Outta touch most of the time') and the corrupt state of the world ('Black is white and white is black/ Got politicians smokin' crack'). It's neither coherent nor artful, but feels like an apt eulogy for the Hagar-fronted band, encapsulating both the personality clash between Eddie and Sammy, and the bitter experience of feeling outdated in the strange new world of the mid-nineties. The song begins as a sombre vocal and guitar duet in bluesy B minor, with soft vocal harmonies joining in the latter stages. The full band crashes in noisily for the chorus, setting up a steady, hammering groove that persists through the next verse. At the three-minute mark, Eddie introduces a new riff that leads into a fine, fierce solo, backed by a thunderous, galloping rhythm section. A slightly awkward gear change returns us to the pounding, slower groove for the extended out-chorus, with layered rhythm guitars joined by ethereal synth strings. This section, with its weighty, churning riff and chiming minor-key arpeggios, is like a rhythmically squared-off version of the outro to The Beatles' 1969 epic, 'I Want You (She's so Heavy)'. However, instead of abruptly cutting out at its zenith like the Beatles' track, 'Feelin'' simmers down, ending with a gentle solo guitar. There's some clumsiness in the execution, especially the messy transitions between sections, but 'Feelin'' still packs considerable punch, providing a powerful ending to the album and a fitting, if bleak, swansong for the first iteration of Van Hagar.

'Crossing Over' [Japanese CD only] (Van Halen, Van Halen, Hagar, Anthony)

This dark, unusual track was originally recorded as a demo by Eddie in 1983. Entitled 'David's Tune', it addressed the suicide of a close friend. Not considered suitable for Van Halen at the time, it languished in the vaults for years. However, following the passing of the band's beloved manager, Ed Leffler, Hagar expressed an interest in recording a version of the song. Unusually, rather than starting from scratch, the band opted to use Eddie's original demo as a foundation, overdubbing more instruments onto his solo recording. Eddie's entire demo, including his programmed drums and original vocal can be heard in the left channel. Alex plays live drums on the right, and Sammy's new lead vocal takes centre stage, interacting interestingly with Eddie's original lines. Eddie, meanwhile, adds layers of harmony guitars to the original demo's ghostly tremolo throb. Sammy's lyrics deal with the concept of reaching 'across to the other side', contacting a lost loved one. This is mirrored in the recording, with Sammy reaching across time to duet with the Eddie of an earlier era. The effect is haunting, unsettling, and unlike anything else in the band's discography.

The song was added to the Japanese CD as an incentive to buy, after imported copies of *Balance* caused offence with the cover's depiction of conjoined twins in a ravaged landscape. This stirred up memories of birth deformities linked to the use of Agent Orange by US forces in Vietnam, which had been extensively covered by the Japanese media. The cover of the Japanese release was hastily altered to show just a single child, and the extra track was added as a bonus. 'Crossing Over' also had a domestic release as the B-side of the 'Can't Stop Lovin' You' single, making it the only non-LP B-side of the band's career.

Best Of: Volume I

Personnel:
Dave Lee Roth: lead vocals
Sammy Hagar: lead vocals
Edward Van Halen: guitar, keyboards, backing vocals
Michael Anthony: bass, backing vocals
Alex Van Halen: drums
Record label: Warner Brothers
Release date: 22 October 1996
Highest chart position: US: 1, UK: 45
Running time: 71:33
Current edition: Rhino Records CD reissue
Tracklisting: 'Eruption', 'Ain't Talkin' 'Bout Love', 'Runnin' with the Devil', 'Dance the Night Away', 'And the Cradle will Rock...', 'Unchained', 'Jump', 'Panama', 'Why Can't This Be Love', 'Dreams', 'When It's Love', 'Poundcake', 'Right Now', 'Can't Stop Lovin' You', 'Humans Being', 'Can't Get This Stuff No More', 'Me Wise Magic'

In 1996, after years of resisting, the band finally released a 'Best of' compilation. Packaged in a sombre black sleeve, with no photos except a black and white shot of their practice space, it seemed perversely calculated to undersell Van Halen's colourful legacy, giving no indication of the larger-than-life delights contained therein. The chronologically ordered tracklisting was largely as expected, although there were a few questionable decisions, such as the absence of anything from *Diver Down*. The real story of the album was the inclusion of two new recordings by the original line-up. According to Hagar, the plan had been to include new songs with both singers, a suggestion which hastened his departure. Dave, meanwhile, was keen to make peace with the band. His solo career had faltered in recent years, and he was happy to be asked to work on new material. Accounts of the abortive reunion vary. Eddie insisted he was very clear that Roth's return was solely for this one-off recording project, while Dave felt that he and the public were led on by the possibility of a full-blown reunion. The press pushed the reunion speculation, although matters were complicated by leaked reports that the band were also auditioning other singers – a rumour later borne out by a leaked recording of them playing 'Panama' with Mitch Malloy in the summer of 1996.

Nevertheless, the band pressed on with publicity for the compilation, including an infamous appearance at the MTV Video Music Awards. Interviewers wanted to know what the future held for the band, and while Roth was enthusiastic, the Van Halen brothers were cagey, with a sullen Eddie refusing to commit to more than the two songs already recorded. Soon the whole thing fell apart as it became clear there were no long-term plans to continue with Roth, and several more years of very public bitterness ensued. In November 1996, former Extreme singer Gary Cherone, another client of manager Ray Danniels was announced as the new vocalist, having been quietly hired before the debacle with Roth unfolded.

'Humans Being' (Van Halen, Van Halen, Hagar, Anthony)

The final song recorded during Sammy's first tenure with the band, 'Humans Being' was written for the *Twister* soundtrack, and its fraught creation accelerated Hagar's exit from the band. Sammy and Eddie's accounts differ significantly. In *Red,* Hagar claims he spoke to the film's director, Jan de Bont, who sent him a copy of the script for lyrical inspiration. Sammy came up with a song called 'Drop Down', which took its title from a piece of the script's twister-chasing jargon. He says, 'the director loved it, told me I told the whole story in three minutes'. Interestingly, in a 1997 *Guitar World* interview, Hagar gave a different account, giving his original title as 'The Silent Extreme', and claiming the song had 'absolutely nothing to do with tornadoes', despite lyrics like 'Sky turning black, knuckles turning white/ Headed for the suck-zone'. By contrast, in *Eruption*, Eddie recalls de Bont specifically asking that the song should *not* be about tornadoes and should 'be reflective of the emotions of the characters', but that Sammy ignored his wishes, requesting a list of tornado-related terms. Whatever the truth, by this stage, the band were clearly no longer communicating effectively. Fuelled by this bitter experience, Hagar went back to the drawing board, and, with (uncredited) assistance from producer, Bruce Fairbairn, produced a new set of startlingly misanthropic lyrics: 'Spread your disease like lemmings breeding/ That's what makes us humans being'. As a song, it's a mixed bag; the main riff is utterly generic, and the verse is a tuneless caveman bellow, closer to the burgeoning nu-metal movement than the traditional Van Halen sound. On the other hand, the chorus provides some much-needed melody and harmony, and Eddie has some fine moments, including a gentle, lyrical mid-tempo solo. Still, it's not a happy listen, and as Hagar screams himself hoarse over the fade-out, his frustration and disillusionment are palpable.

'Can't Get This Stuff No More' (Van Halen, Van Halen, Roth, Anthony)

Given the anticipation and hype surrounding the reunion of the original line-up, you might expect their first recorded offering to be explosive. Instead, 'Can't Get This Stuff No More' begins tentatively with gentle guitar arpeggios before settling into a moderately-rocking 6/8 shuffle. Eddie's riff uses his favourite trick of moving chord shapes around over a fixed pedal point – in this case, moving a D major up two frets to make an E and E sus5 – but it's restrained compared to the cocksure flash of old. Roth immediately sounds at home on the sultry blues of the verse, his higher register still fairly intact and his growling lower range developing nicely. The chorus is more melodic, adding pleasing harmonies. The track's main surprise comes in the first half of the guitar solo, which finds Eddie using a talk-box for the first time. This device sends the guitar's sound along a tube, allowing the player to shape the sound with their mouth, and project it into a vocal mic. It was first popularised by Peter Frampton and later used by Ritchie Sambora on Bon Jovi's hit, 'Livin' on a Prayer' (1986). Dave really unleashes on a final chorus, but rather than end there, the track carries on with another minute and a half of muted noodling, somewhat diminishing its impact.

According to Dave, there was considerable friction around the lyric writing process, with the brothers rejecting his ideas and trying to push him into performing material they had already written with producer Glenn Ballard (then riding high on the success of Alanis Morissette's *Jagged Little Pill* (1995)) and Desmond Child, a songwriter whose credits include massive hits for Bon Jovi, Kiss, and Aerosmith. Roth suffered through this indignity, eventually managing to get his own words onto the new tracks. 'Can't Get This Stuff No More' opens with a little old-school Roth *braggadocio* ('Got me a date with a supermodel'). However, it doesn't develop into a lurid tale of the narrator's exploits. Instead, the lyrics offer a wry, somewhat bitter summary of Roth's feelings about the circumstances of the reunion. The chorus especially seems to directly reflect Roth's feeling that he has been misled by the band and concludes with a warning: 'Keep that in mind when we say goodbye/ 'Cuz you can't get this stuff no more' – the 'stuff' in question being his own talent and charisma. It's not the most immediate Van Halen song, paling in comparison to the earlier Roth tunes on the compilation. Nevertheless, it's a grower, and though it may lack the pizzaz of the band's classics, it has considerably more substance than the filler material that padded out the more recent Van Hagar albums.

'Me Wise Magic' (Van Halen, Van Halen, Roth, Anthony)

The harder-rocking of the two new tracks, *Me Wise Magic,* kicks off with a softly brooding riff based on an awkward nine-beat phrase. The TransTrem system, last heard on *5150,* makes a reappearance, sending the final chord of a phrase plunging before a proggy flourish introduces the song proper. The track has a hard, funky groove, driven by Eddie's restless rhythm playing, packed with the dazzling, flashy touches that were conspicuously absent from the previous track. Roth takes the verses in a close-miked low drawl, before belting out the bridge in his upper register. There's a psychedelic touch, with the line 'I am you and you are me' fed through a rotating Leslie speaker effect, emphasising the lyric's trippy nature. The chorus is expansive, with huge open chords and a prominent backing vocal maintaining a high B drone throughout. A sizzling wah-wah solo is particularly notable for the culminating, rhythmically perplexing jazz/prog passage, showing that years of cranking out soft-rock hits haven't dulled the brothers' taste for the musically obtuse. The shred-heavy out-chorus leads back to a reprise of the intro, now with added tapped harmonics, bringing this storming rocker to a sombre end.

Glen Ballard had already written lyrics to the song before Roth came on board, but Dave rewrote them to better suit his personality. The mystical theme is atypical for Roth, who prefers to couch his philosophical musings in more outwardly prosaic lyrics. It's metaphysical stuff, with the narrative voice alternating between an omnipotent power and a human being on a spiritual quest before revealing that they are one and the same. Deep, eh? Still, in case it all sounds too portentous, Roth is happy to point out the disposable, meaninglessness of it all: 'My words at best to you a fortune coo-coo-cookie'. Roth's blend of wry self-deprecation and zen self-abnegation keeps the lyric from tipping into out-and-out pomposity. At over six minutes, it's the longest song ever recorded by the original line-up. It could have been tightened up with editing, but remains a powerful piece of work, despite the unpleasant circumstances surrounding its creation.

Van Halen III (1998)

Personnel:
Gary Cherone: lead vocals
Edward Van Halen: guitar, bass guitar, keyboards, drums, electric sitar, lead vocals on 'How Many Say I', backing vocals
Michael Anthony: bass, backing vocals
Alex Van Halen: drums
Additional personnel:
Mike Post: piano on 'Neworld'
Recorded at 5150 Studios, Studio City, March – December 1997
Produced by Mike Post and Edward Van Halen
Engineered by Erwin Musper
Record label: Warner Brothers
Release date: 17 March, 1998
Highest chart position: US: 4, UK: 43
Running time: 65:22
Current edition: 1998 CD/ Rhino Records 2017 mp3 reissue

Although he was already lined up before Roth returned for the *Best Of* album, Gary Cherone was finally announced as the new lead singer of Van Halen in November 1996, While he wasn't the big name Hagar had been prior to joining the band, there was a logic to his appointment. He had a proven track record with Extreme, whose Van Halen-meets-Queen sound had brought them considerable success before the grunge explosion rendered them hopelessly out-of-touch overnight. He was a perfectly competent singer, but not a big personality like Roth or Hagar had been, and was happy to be a supporting player in Eddie and Alex's band. Eddie was impressed with his thoughtful writing style and by the fact that he would provide lyrics for the guitarist to set to music rather than working the other way round. Instead of touring to allow the new vocalist to settle in (something Cherone later regretted they had not done), the band opted to get straight to work on new music. Eddie was in apparently high spirits. He had been working with therapist/guru Sat-Kaur Khalsa on his sobriety and mental health and was enjoying a spell of unfettered creativity. However, interviews from the time reveal a strained, manic quality to his spiritual well-being. This quality carries over into the album's music, with tracks overflowing with ideas, haphazardly thrown together with little thought of refinement or editing.

Rather than hiring a name producer like Ballard or Fairbairn, Eddie opted to use his friend Mike Post, an accomplished composer for the screen but not particularly known for his production work, especially in a heavy rock context. He was content to take a back seat, functioning more as an engineer than producer, and didn't provide the discipline or guidance needed to hone the album into a listenable, coherent product. Eddie dominates the record, his guitar running roughshod over every track, while Michael Anthony was almost completely side-lined. He was only allowed to play on three of the 12 tracks, with Eddie handling the bass for the remainder, and even his trademark backing vocals are largely absent. The resulting album was a confusing, disheartening product. There were some fantastic ideas, but they were too often lost amid overlong, sloppily arranged tracks. Poor Gary Cherone didn't stand a chance, with few memorable hooks in the entire 65-minute marathon and a mix that presented his vocal in a harsh light, rendering his voice thin and grating. Even the cover – a grainy stock photo of vaudevillian Frank Richards being hit by a cannonball – seemed ill-conceived and dreary, with a terrible, cheap-looking font. The title was a bold statement, placing the album on a par with the band's epochal first brace of LPs while announcing the beginning of a third major phase. Unfortunately, the public weren't buying it, literally or figuratively. It reached number four on the *Billboard* chart but drastically underperformed compared to the band's previous efforts and received largely negative reviews. The failure of the album was a crushing blow to Eddie, who felt it was among his best work. With his self-confidence spiralling and a series of personal issues and health setbacks overwhelming him, it would be many years before he would feel ready to make another new Van Halen LP.

'Neworld' (Van Halen, Van Halen, Cherone, Anthony)
The third phase of Van Halen begins with this out-of-character pastoral instrumental waltz. Played as a duet between Eddie's acoustic guitar and a piano, played by producer Mike Post, the track has a delicate, folky feel – not unlike latter-day Fairport Convention. Eddie's playing contains a couple of recognisable Van Halen touches, particularly when he takes over the melody on harmonics, and there's a hint of ominous dissonance in Post's heavy bass notes towards the end. Otherwise, it's mellow, verging on twee. A curious choice to open the record – one of many the band made in this era.

'Without You' (Van Halen, Van Halen, Cherone, Anthony)
After the somnolent 'Neworld', the album proper begins with 'Without You'. The loose-limbed groove, and choppy, relatively clean-toned rhythm guitar create a hard funk sound, similar to the style of Cherone's former band, Extreme, or even the Red Hot Chilli Peppers. The verses are hard-driving, rhythmic and bluesy, leading onto a psychedelic bridge section, complete with Beatles-y harmonies and trippy Leslie effects. The chorus is big, open and melodic. It's catchy but cries out for Mike's harmony, which is sadly absent. Nevertheless, the song's building blocks are fundamentally sound, and with Eddie playing with renewed fire and invention, should make for a decent, if not classic record. Unfortunately, two significant issues prevent this. Firstly, there's a palpable lack of attention to small, important details; a mellow middle-eight is marred by an out-of-tune lead overdub; several of

Cherone's high notes are noticeably flat – not because he can't sing them, but because no one bothered to get him to record a better take; and the unforgiving mix sabotages the hapless singer, leaving his voice sounding exposed, dry and trebly. Secondly, there's just too much of it; Eddie needed someone with the forceful personality and solid commercial instincts of Roth or Templeman to counterbalance his wilder indulgences. Without that balance, a perfectly serviceable three-minute song becomes a stodgy six-and-a-half-minute string of riffs. The lyrics are an uninspiring depiction of a failing relationship, possibly conceived as a comment on either Hagar or Roth's bitter departure from the band. Eddie had a hand in the lyric writing process on this track, although the extent of his contribution is unclear, with the guitarist claiming in *Eruption* that he wrote 'the first two verses and the chorus', while Cherone only recalls Eddie (and Alex too) pitching in on the chorus. 'Without You' has the makings of a good track but is somehow simultaneously over- and under-done. Still, aided by a tremendously expensive video, the single managed to debut at number one in the *Billboard* Mainstream Rock chart, although it didn't threaten the sales-based Hot 100.

'One I Want' (Van Halen, Van Halen, Cherone, Anthony)

With its reggae-tinged rhythm section and clean-toned rhythm guitar, 'One I Want' feels closer to The Police, circa 'Roxanne' (1978) than the traditional Van Halen sound. Even Cherone's vocals sound remarkably Sting-like, which is not necessarily a bad thing but suggests that the new line-up was experiencing an identity crisis. The call and response verses feature the backing vocals (overdubbed by Cherone, rather than being sung by Eddie and Mike), singing the first part of each phrase, answered by the lead. The reggae-ish feel gives way to a straight up-tempo beat for the bridge and chorus, with Eddie cranking up the overdrive for the chorus. The great, intricate rhythm guitar parts on these sections are let down by the weak, nebulous vocal melody, which sounds as though Gary is just wailing and hoping to hit a note that fits, with mixed results. The chorus backing vocals are jarring too, with their first and third lines clashing with the backing track. Again, Mike's voice is nowhere to be heard, and would certainly have helped. The lyrics use a simple list formula. The backing vocals name a type of '-man' ('Superman'). The lead responds by telling us what or who this man wants ('He lookin' for Lois'). Devices like this have been used by songwriters since time immemorial, and can be effective if executed with wit and economy. However, here, the concept feels underdeveloped. We quickly get the idea – different men want different things, but the narrator just wants you – but there are still another two long verses to slog through. Add to that a lengthy guitar solo, where eight or 16 bars would have been ideal, and you're overstretching a very slight concept. There are some interesting touches, but they don't cohere into a satisfying song.

'From Afar' (Van Halen, Van Halen, Cherone, Anthony)

More bizarre choices are in evidence here. This eerily empty recording consists largely of Gary's voice and Eddie's echo-laden guitar, with Alex spending lengthy spells merely keeping time on his hi-hat and adding occasional pompous timpani rolls. The lyrics are a meditation on isolation and separation from a loved one, which the track's sparseness is presumably intended to reflect. Unfortunately, neither the melody or lyrics are particularly engaging, and Cherone's pitchy, straining vocal is unflatteringly exposed. Things pick up a little from the middle eight when a regular drumbeat finally settles in. There's a fun instrumental with wildly panning guitars, a fine solo and some sixties-style flanging over the final chorus. However, it's telling that the song's tricks and effects remain in the memory more than the melody or lyrics. 'From Afar' is really little more than five-and-a-half minutes of sonic gimmickry in search of a song.

'Dirty Water Dog' (Van Halen, Van Halen, Cherone, Anthony)

I've had harsh words to say about a few of Sammy's lyrics, but on 'Dirty Water Dog', Cherone outdoes even Hagar's worst efforts. The verses at least attempt to be thoughtful, exploring the narrator's views on politics and religion: 'Position's always been a little left of cynical/ I'm fundamentally for the individual'. The rhyme scheme and scansion are haphazard, but at least there appears to be a point. Unfortunately, the song goes completely off the rails in the chorus, suddenly becoming an anthem to voyeurism, with surely the worst lines in the entire Van Halen canon: 'Sometimes a certain tom's gotta peep/ I'm a peek-a-boy, lookin' at girls'. It may be intended as tongue-in-cheek humour, *ala* Roth, but the effect is creepy and unpleasant. The absence of a musical hook doesn't help, either. The vocal line meanders aimlessly on the blues scale, and the track lacks a strong, memorable riff. The main rhythm guitar has a clean, heavily-chorused sound, which feels very 1980s. Eddie's playing is intricate, restlessly shifting between blues licks, melodic arpeggios and prog flourishes, never settling into a steady pattern. Though overly busy, it does at least distract attention from the forgettable melody and abysmal lyric. Elsewhere, there's another fine solo, built on long, arcing vibrato bar dives. Eddie also plays some solid bass, although it's nothing Anthony couldn't have handled, suggesting his exclusion was for personal rather than musical reasons. Again, it's a frustrating record, with intriguing musical ingredients wasted on a poor song.

'Once' (Van Halen, Van Halen, Cherone, Anthony)

Another un-Van Halen-like track, 'Once' is a sprawling ballad, stretched out to almost eight minutes. Neither Michael nor Alex feature on the track, with programmed percussion in place of live drums and Eddie playing synth bass, piano and several layers of electric and acoustic guitars. There are a couple of intriguing ideas, notably a solo that appears to be played on a baritone guitar, with a booming Duane Eddy-like low twang that cuts nicely through the airbrushed backing. For the most part, though, this is soft-focus elevator music. The lyrics do nothing to justify the song's existence, either. They strive for profundity but end up as another list-making exercise like 'One I Want'. Cherone establishes a formula for each line of the verses, then it's simply a matter of filling in the blanks: 'Once born, can't ever be not conceived/ Once present, can't ever be past/ Once first, can't ever be not ever last'. It's pretentious, meaningless, and frequently veers into gibberish in order to scan or rhyme. Overall, a massively overlong and insipid outing that has no business calling itself a Van Halen song and a low point on an album of few highs.

'Fire in the Hole' (Van Halen, Van Halen, Cherone, Anthony)

This is a bit more like it! With a souped-up AC/DC riff interspersed with great, imaginative fills and the Alex and Mike rhythm section back together, 'Fire in the Hole' has the feel of a 'proper' Van Halen song. There's a catchy sing-along chorus, which is a rarity on this LP. Again, it's very AC/DC-like, but that's no bad thing. Indeed, the similarity to the antipodean legends benefits Cherone, his harsh vocal possessing a Brian Johnson-like quality that suits this track better than most of the album's other songs. His tongue-twisting lyrics are the only element that doesn't fit the back-to-basics feel. Thematically, the song is a condemnation of someone given to making shocking, explosive statements – the 'Fire in the Hole' of the title. To illustrate this, Gary weaves a web of convoluted mixed metaphors, using imagery from dentistry, equestrianism, maritime themes and more, inventing the word 'decavities' in the process. It's entertainingly ludicrous, which would be okay if the intent was humorous, but Cherone is apparently entirely serious. Nevertheless, the track is a highlight of the album, with excellent Trans-Trem guitar work and a solidly rocking performance all round. The final minute, which features a couple of new riffs over a drum loop and background CB radio chatter, is unnecessary, though, bloating the track with excess material to its detriment. Still, 'Fire in the Hole' shows welcome signs of life amid a desolate album.

'Josephina' (Van Halen, Van Halen, Cherone, Anthony)

'Josephina' is an odd blend of elements. It has one foot in the mawkish acoustic balladry that gave Cherone's previous band, Extreme, a huge hit with 'More Than Words' (1991). At the same time, the track's unorthodox rhythmic and harmonic twists and turns mark it as progressive rock. From a saccharine opening, the song builds in toughness and momentum as Alex's drums enter, with Eddie blending hints of electric guitar in with his double-tracked acoustics. His solo is impressive, building from an 'Intruder'-like barrage of shrieks and rattles to a soaring, swooping melodic line. There's not much of a hook – the closest thing being the repeated refrain of 'Can you shine a light?', although catchiness presumably wasn't the main priority of this strange puzzle of a song. Cherone shows a softer side in the acoustic setting, though reverts to a top-of-the-lungs screech for the louder sections. His lyrics are atypical hard rock fare, addressing an elderly relative or friend, encouraging her to reminisce about her younger days and 'shine a light' on her past. It's quite a sweet concept, although sections are clumsily written, forcing Cherone into a garbled half-spoken delivery to make the words fit. Also, when the narrator imagines young Josephina 'breaking hearts' with 'Pigtails and painted toes, all dressed up in your mother's clothes', the effect is more creepy than nostalgic. The nostalgia is reinforced at the track's end, when Eddie's gentle acoustic fades, leaving the sound of a fairground calliope, evoking long-lost childhood memories. 'Josephina' is an attempt at something different, and not completely without merit. However, it feels like a failed experiment, leaving one pining for the catchy, carefree band of old. Cherone, interviewed for an interlude in *Eruption* concurs, cheekily blaming Mike Post in the process: 'A producer might've heard 'Josephina' and said, 'Yeah, Okay. Let's put that over on the side – we need a rocker'.

'Year to the Day' (Van Halen, Van Halen, Cherone, Anthony)

Of all *Van Halen III*'s myriad flaws, its tendency towards excruciatingly over-extended songs if perhaps the worst. 'Year to the Day' is a case in point – a two-verse minor-key blues in slow 6/8, dragged out beyond eight torturous minutes. There are strong precedents for hard rock bands playing extended minor blues songs, notably Led Zeppelin's towering 'Since I've Been Loving You' (1970). Unfortunately, 'Year to the Day' totally lacks that track's soul and heart-stopping dynamics. Instead, it veers awkwardly between quiet guitar/ vocal verses and screeching, blaring choruses, with no middle ground. The drum-less sections are dominated by Eddie's fussy neo-baroque twiddling, with Cherone's vocal wafting around in vain search for a tune. At the end of the verse, the track halts, restarting as pounding, unsubtle rock, with a harsh guitar tone and unpleasantly grating vocal. There's some fire in Eddie's solo, but like everything else, it's overextended. He builds from a murmur to a scream but then just keeps screaming with nowhere else to go. The lyrics recall the loss of a loved one, either due to the end of a relationship, or, as verse two hints, through death. The chorus conveys this in a clear, if perfunctory way: 'A year to the day since you went away/ A moment in time when you were last mine'. You'd expect the verses to fill in the story, but instead, Gary gets so tangled in a mess of metaphors and similes that he tells us nothing at all: 'Crop is gone, left only chaff/ A bitter pill, and an overcast/ A flag unfurled at half-mast'. It's a weak song, gruellingly over-long, and sonically unappealing. A definite miss, then.

'Primary' (Van Halen, Van Halen, Cherone, Anthony)

This brief, off-the-cuff instrumental is one of the album's most enjoyable tracks. It features Eddie on the Coral electric sitar, an instrument not heard on a Van Halen record since 'Ain't Talkin' 'Bout Love'. He uses a sparkling clean, chorused sound, with his low E string tuned down to A, creating an octave pairing on the bottom two strings. Not remotely Indian-sounding, the piece is built on wonderful slip-sliding blues lines peppered with pinging harmonics, which sound otherworldly with the added resonance of the instrument's drone strings. There's an *audio verité* quality to the recording, which includes the sound of the sitar being plugged in, and various ambient clicks, buzzes and hisses. This gives the impression that someone just happened to press record, capturing a moment of genius by chance. It's a fleeting but welcome reminder of Eddie's monumental talent on an album during which he often seems to have lost his way.

'Ballot or the Bullet' (Van Halen, Van Halen, Cherone, Anthony)
Eddie had expressed a desire for Van Halen's lyrics to address more serious topics, and Gary obliges on 'Ballot or the Bullet', a well-meaning but clumsy and misguided evocation of the famous speech given by Malcolm X on 3 April 1964 at the Cory Methodist Church in Cleveland, Ohio, and again at the King Solomon Baptist Church, Detroit, Michigan on the 12th. The fierce, witty and wide-ranging speech covered issues of human rights and X's dedication to black nationalism. The crux of the speech was that, if politicians' promises on civil rights were not met, a violent response from African-American communities would become inevitable:

> It's time for you and me to become more politically mature and realise what a ballot is for, and that if we don't cast a ballot, it's going to end up in a situation where we're going to have to cast a bullet.

Cherone tries to compress the message of X's 50-minute speech into a five-minute song. Unfortunately, the snippets of X's words, filtered through Cherone's questionable interpretive lens, lose their nuance and power. Without the context of the civil rights struggle, the song could just as easily be calling for a right-wing libertarian uprising as advocating for black power.

Musically, it's pulverising heavy metal – all crunching down-tuned riffs and hammering double-kicks. The main riff is terrific, landing somewhere between the dark sound of *Fair Warning* and the contemporary heavy grunge of Alice in Chains. The bridge kicks into double time, and adds ringing chords while vocal harmonies embellish the chorus. Unfortunately, the chorus hook is weak, and the faster tempo dissipates the power of the verses. Again, Cherone's voice sounds dry and exposed in the mix, which doesn't help. There's a post-chorus blast of Son House-style slashing acoustic slide blues, which is a nice touch, breaking up the punishing wall of noise. This makes a reappearance later, concluding a track that shows promise, but is hampered by ham-fisted lyrics and the absence of a decent hook.

121

'How Many Say I' (Van Halen, Van Halen, Cherone, Anthony)

The album closes with one of the band's most unusual tracks. 'How Many Say I' is a slow piano ballad featuring Eddie's only lead vocal performance on record. Although both critics and fans reacted largely negatively to the whole album, their bitterest ire was reserved for this track, with much of the criticism aimed at Eddie's vocal. By this stage, he no longer has the bright, clear voice that blended so well with Mike's on those early records. Decades of chain-smoking and alcohol abuse have left him with a low, fractured growl. However, though raw, there's a heart-breaking vulnerability and tenderness to Eddie's performance. Cherone, in his *Eruption* interlude, compares Eddie's singing to Tom Waits and Pink Floyd's Roger Waters, both apt comparisons. His husky, fragile tones are perfectly suited to the introspective lyrics, which find him confronting a list of personal failings, and which are married to an affecting melody. It's worlds away from the traditional Van Halen sound, which presumably deterred many listeners immediately. However, the song did find a few fans, notably *Rolling Stone*'s Greg Kott, who, while dismissing the album as a whole, praised Eddie's 'disarmingly appealing, nicotine-stained voice', with good reason. It's not all positive, of course. Like the whole album, 'How Many Say I' is over-stretched and doesn't benefit from the slickly-dramatic arrangement, with added strings and woodwind. A simpler vocal and piano arrangement would have been more impactful, but looking past the bells and whistles, there's a simple, naked honesty to the song that makes it much more satisfying than most of the rest of the album.

The Best of Both Worlds (2004)

Personnel:
Dave Lee Roth: lead vocals
Sammy Hagar: lead vocals
Edward Van Halen: guitar, keyboards, backing vocals
Michael Anthony: bass, backing vocals
Alex Van Halen: drums
Additional personnel:
Steve Lukather: backing vocals (tracks 2-4, 14 on disc one, track 10 on disc two)
Record label: Warner Brothers
Release date: 20 July 2004
Highest chart position: US: 3, UK: 15
Running time: 156:57
Current edition: Rhino Records CD reissue
Tracklisting: Disc one: 'Eruption', 'It's About Time', 'Up For Breakfast', 'Learning to See', 'Ain't Talkin' 'Bout Love', 'Finish What Ya Started', 'You Really Got Me', 'Dreams', 'Hot For Teacher', 'Poundcake', 'And the Cradle will Rock...', 'Black and Blue', 'Jump', 'Top of the World', '(Oh) Pretty Woman', 'Love Walks In', 'Beautiful Girls', 'Can't Stop Lovin' You', 'Unchained'
Disc two: 'Panama', 'Best of Both Worlds', 'Jamie's Cryin'', 'Runaround', 'I'll Wait', 'Why Can't This Be Love', 'Runnin' with the Devil', 'When It's Love', 'Dancing in the Street', 'Strung Out/ Not Enough', 'Feels so Good', 'Right Now', 'Everybody Wants Some!', 'Dance the Night Away', 'Ain't Talkin' 'Bout Love (Live)', 'Panama (Live)', 'Jump (Live)'

Van Halen were in the wilderness in the early 2000s. A second album with Gary Cherone had been started, but poor record sales, declining concert attendances and record company pressure led to the singer's amicable departure. There followed some difficult years, during which Eddie endured a battle with tongue cancer and the breakdown of his marriage. During this period, another reunion with Roth was attempted, getting as far as cutting some new demos before tensions resurfaced and everything fell apart again. Although the band had made a vast fortune over the years, the brothers had not invested wisely, and with expensive divorces looming, needed to generate income. The obvious move was to approach Sammy Hagar, who had recently unexpectedly co-headlined with Roth on the so-called 'Sam and Dave' tour, a momentous clash of monster egos if ever there was one. Hagar had diversified, starting several successful businesses, including the popular Cabo Wabo tequila brand, so didn't have the pressing need for a reunion that the Van Halens did. Nevertheless, his manager saw the potential rewards of re-joining the band, and reached out to Alex to set things in motion. A plan was hatched for a new, more comprehensive 'best of' collection and accompanying tour. For the compilation, they would record three new songs, with Glen Ballard returning to produce.

When Hagar arrived at 5150 to work on the new material, he found Eddie at his lowest ebb. Paranoid, skittish and unstable, he was living like a vagrant, rarely washing or changing his clothes, his teeth blackened by his new habit of drinking cheap red wine from the bottle. The writing and recording sessions were torturous, with Eddie unable to stay focused for long enough to complete a take, yet insisting on playing bass as well as guitar and keyboards. Somehow, the three songs were eventually completed, with Anthony returning to record backing vocals at Sammy's insistence. The double CD was released, and the band toured to promote it. Eddie was not in a suitable physical or mental condition to undertake a gruelling tour, but with so much money at stake, the machine rolled on. As Sammy demanded, Anthony played in the touring line-up but was effectively reduced to being a salaried employee of the band he had loyally served in for nearly 30 years. Performances were often erratic, with Eddie clearly struggling to remain sober, not helped by Hagar's callous determination to use every available opportunity to plug his tequila. Inevitably, the tour ended in bitter acrimony, and neither Hagar nor Anthony would take the stage as members of Van Halen again.

The compilation is far better packaged than *Best Of: Volume I* and corrects some of its omissions by including songs from *Diver Down* and some favourite non-single tracks. Still, the sequencing is odd. The three new songs are sandwiched together between 'Eruption' and 'Ain't Talkin' ' Bout Love', inevitably suffering by comparison. The choice of a non-chronological track list is bold, and throws up interesting juxtapositions, but doesn't always do the songs a great service. For instance, if you didn't already think 'Dreams' was weak and vapid, try hearing it in between 'You Really Got Me' and 'Hot For Teacher'. It's understandable that nothing from the unloved *Van Halen III* made the cut, but the inclusion of three Hagar-sung 'live' versions of Roth-era classics is baffling when the vastly superior original recordings already feature earlier on the record. The album sold well and kept Van Halen in the public consciousness, but the tour did little to help their reputation, and with Hagar's swift departure, the band's future looked very uncertain indeed.

'It's About Time' (Van Halen, Van Halen, Hagar)

The first of the new tracks is promising: a lively number with a classic Van Halen feel, wedded to a more contemporary down-tuned weightiness. Hagar's lyrics are almost too on-the-nose as an assertion that the band are putting their mistakes behind them and getting back to what they do best, even referencing Eddie's famous colour scheme: 'Turn your clock back/ Paint it red on black/ We'll get it all right back'. The guitars sound powerful and chunky and are doubled in a stereo pair, rather than using different tracks for rhythm and lead. It's not an approach Eddie has taken before, but it works well here. There's a reasonably catchy chorus, aided by the welcome return of Mike's voice (Anthony, notably, is not listed in the writing credits for the first time on these new tracks). The instrumental includes some enjoyably brutal riffing, and a superbly crafted solo before a frantic final chorus leads to a traditional stadium rock crash ending. Hagar's corny, nostalgia-heavy lyrics may not be his best work, but they do the job, and considering the difficult circumstances surrounding its creation, this is a remarkably assured return to form.

'Up For Breakfast' (Van Halen, Van Halen, Hagar)
Nearly 20 years after the cringe-worthy food/sex metaphors of 'Good Enough', Sammy seems to be trying to outdo himself with 'Up For Breakfast'. While lyrics like 'Put that butter on my biscuit, honey to my melons/ Woo, put berries on my bananas, I need a second helping' might have passed in the mid-eighties, they don't cut it in the 21st century. There's very little melody, and no notable hook to make the track memorable, although Anthony's backing vocals at least add a hint of pop. It's a shame 'Up for Breakfast' is such a weak song, as there are some cool musical ideas in the background, from the pulsing, propulsive synth to Eddie's restlessly inventive rhythm playing. If anything, it suffers from the same issue as many *Van Halen III* tracks, with so many riffs crammed into the song that it never settles into a familiar, memorable pattern. Still, if you can overlook Hagar's dreadful words, 'Up for Breakfast' is a decent blast of mid-tempo raunchiness. It's just a pity that it's sequenced just before a huge list of songs that make it seem hopelessly weak by comparison.

'Learning to See' (Van Halen, Van Halen, Hagar)
The third new song is the longest, darkest and heaviest of the bunch. The deceptively mellow verses, with their tinkling harmonics, lull the listener into a sense of security, but the chorus is pure churning anguish. Eddie manages to wring some melodic lines out of his guitar amid the heavily distorted detuned sludge, while Sammy howls words of deep regret: 'I didn't see you fallin'/ I never heard you callin''. We might imagine that the song is his response to Eddie's harrowing struggle with addiction, but given the lack of compassion he expresses towards the guitarist in *Red*, this seems doubtful. A particularly aggressive solo finds Eddie layering two tracks of machine-gun shredding and screaming divebombed harmonics, creating a sensation akin to being caught in an air raid. It's powerful stuff, with an emotional intensity that becomes almost overbearing towards the end, with Eddie's lead shrieking wildly, and Hagar abandoning words for unhinged primal screams. Not a fun, comfortable listen, but a worthy addition to the catalogue, and certainly better than 'Up for Breakfast'.

A Different Kind of Truth (2012)

Personnel:
David Lee Roth: lead vocals, synthesiser on 'Tattoo', acoustic guitar on 'Stay Frosty'
Edward Van Halen: guitar, backing vocals
Wolfgang Van Halen: bass, backing vocals, additional guitar on 'China Town'
Alex Van Halen: drums
Recorded at 5150 and Henson Recording Studios, Hollywood, November 2010 – January 2012
Produced by Van Halen and John Shanks
Engineered by Martin Cooke
Record label: Interscope
Release date: 7 February 2012
Highest chart position: US: 2, UK: 6
Running time: 50:12
Current edition: 2012 CD

Following the debacle of the 2004 tour, Van Halen receded from public view to lick their wounds. Eddie had some demons to battle, and with the brothers losing their mother, Eugenia, in 2005, making music was not their number one priority. There were signs of activity in 2006, however. Firstly, Eddie contributed some music to the score of Michael Ninn's horror-porn film, *The Sacred Sin*. This was an unorthodox choice of project, but at least he was making music again. He also joined forces with Fender on a range of EVH-branded guitars and amps, which were launched the following year, marking the culmination of a lifetime's innovation. Most significant for fans was the announcement in October that his then-16-year-old son, Wolfgang was Van Halen's new bassist. This was met with bafflement and outrage by some fans. Michael Anthony had been a popular, relatable figure and a key part of the band's sound. To replace him with an untried teenager seemed risky at best, and insane at worst. Nevertheless, a 2007 tour was duly announced, with Roth returning as frontman, and the band's performances showed that fans had nothing to fear – Wolfgang was more than capable of handling the material if a little reserved onstage. Furthermore, Eddie was clearly overjoyed to be playing music with his son, seeming healthier and in better spirits than he had in years.

Hurt by negative reactions to the band's more recent recorded output, Eddie was reluctant to follow the tour with a new record. However, at Wolfgang's urging, the band reworked three songs from their early demos to be included as bonus tracks on a proposed compilation of hidden gems and deep cuts. This started the creative juices flowing and reminded the band of other early songs with the potential to be updated. The project soon turned into a new studio album, using early demos as a starting point. At Roth's suggestion, producer John Shanks, mainly known for his work with pop artists like

Ashlee Simpson and Kelly Clarkson, was hired. Roth also suggested recording at Henson Studios, taking the band out of 5150, where they had made every record since *1984,* although they did later retreat to Eddie's studio to re-do some guitar and bass tracks and add finishing touches. The resulting album was a perfect balance between the classic sound of the band's late-seventies records and a more modern sonic blueprint. The reworked material blended seamlessly with the new and was delivered with a vibrancy and joy that had been absent from the last several Van Halen releases. All three Van Halens turned in superb performances, with Eddie back on world-beating form and Wolfgang's huge-sounding authoritative bass work silencing any remaining doubters. Roth might have lost some of his high range and the trademark scream but had gained a rich low-register growl, used effectively on several songs. Most importantly, he was as charismatic as ever and sounded delighted to be back where he belonged. Packaged in a striking red sleeve, featuring the classic winged-VH logo and a looming image of a J-3A steam locomotive, the album was released by a new label, Interscope, the band having parted from Warner Brothers back in 2001. Preceded by the single, 'Tattoo', in January 2012, the album followed in February and was a hit, reaching number two on the *Billboard* chart and six on the UK album chart, their highest ever placing on that side of the pond.

Even critics responded favourably, and fans were hopeful that this could be the beginning of an extended run for the revitalised band. Live shows supporting the album were successful and well attended, although Eddie's health issues caused a number of dates to be cancelled. Nevertheless, having put the petty squabbles and paranoia behind them and collaborating more happily than they had in decades, the band's outlook seemed tentatively optimistic.

'Tattoo' (Van Halen, Roth)

After opening with vocal harmonies treated with reversed echo, 'Tattoo' roars out of the gate with a huge mid-tempo riff. The sound is rich and full, with Wolfgang's bass growling warmly and Roth adding unobtrusive synth chords – his first keyboard performance on a Van Halen record since 'Intruder'. Eddie overdubs a catchy lead hook, and the band sounds sprightlier and more confident than they have in years. The song takes a familiar pattern, with softer, bluesier verses, a more melodic bridge, and a punchy chorus with big harmonies. Without Anthony, these inevitably sound different, but Dave does a great job here, overdubbing his own backing vocals, although Eddie and Wolfgang do contribute elsewhere on the album. The track is based on an early song called 'Down in Flames', a fixture of the band's live sets circa 1977. The original song was fine, but the revised version is tighter and more tuneful, with a new chorus hook and quirkier, less-generic words. Roth's new lyrics explore his long-standing fascination with tattoo culture. Packed with punning wordplay, the song explains the different purposes that skin

127

art can serve; as a means of expressing hidden desires or personality traits, as an autobiographical record, or a means of confirming an affiliation. As we'd expect from Roth, the words are playful on the surface but surprisingly thoughtful on closer inspection. Eddie takes a superb, blazing solo over a verse and a bridge, avoiding the over-extended noodling that bogged down *Van Halen III*. Dave is also on superb form, gleefully selling cornball wordplay ('Mousewife to momshell') while lending unexpected gravitas to the final verse, discussing the symbolic significance of the narrator's uncle's union tattoo. After a wild out-chorus, the track ends with a series of hushed chord swells, referencing the intro to 'Down in Flames', which was also borrowed for the band's cover of 'You're No Good'.

Released as the album's first single, 'Tattoo' brought Van Halen back into the Hot 100 for the first time in 17 years, peaking at number 67 and hit number one on the *Billboard* Hard Rock Digital Songs chart. Wolfgang lobbied for 'She's the Woman' to be the first single, feeling it to be more representative of the album as a whole, but for me, 'Tattoo' was a fine choice – a bold, swaggering return to form, reminding listeners of how exciting and fun a Van Halen record could be.

'She's The Woman' (Van Halen, Roth)

While 'Tattoo' was an excellent opening gambit, Wolfgang wasn't wrong about 'She's the Woman' – it absolutely smokes! The song originally appeared on the 1976 Gene Simmons demo. This reworking keeps the basic structure, riff and chorus but has a new, far superior vocal line and a fresh set of lyrics. It also includes a new instrumental section after the original passage was repurposed as part of 'Mean Street'. The new recording is taken at a slower, less runaway tempo than the original, adding weight and swing. Opening with wailing wah-wah lead over a restless high bass lick, the track soon slips into a killer riff. All three Instrumentalists work brilliantly together, with great guitar and bass interplay and Alex driving everything along with propulsive hi-hat sixteenths. The track is very much in the spirit of the band's debut – a hefty dose of Led Zeppelin flash with a hint of punky sneer. After years of Hagar and Cherone's terrible lyrics about sex, it's wonderful to have Roth back to show us how it's done. 'She's the Woman' is a perfect example of his craft, melding pulp fiction jive and near-the-knuckle wit to create something that sounds risqué, without ever veering into crassness. As he says in the second bridge, 'This song ain't dirty, it's really just the way we sing it'! The instrumental starts with a mean-sounding proggy breakdown, with yowling wah-wah lead panning wildly over slashing riffs and juddering off-beat accents. This builds into an excellent composed melodic lead line, that breaks up the heavy blues feel nicely. Refreshingly, after a final chorus, the song simply slams to a halt, with no drawn-out repetitions or tacked-on sections. It's a breath-taking 2.57 of top-drawer hard rock, made all the more powerful by its brevity – a virtue that the band seemed to have forgotten during more recent years.

'You and Your Blues' (Van Halen, Roth)

The first completely newly written song on the album stands up very well against the reworked older material. It depicts a relationship at breaking point, caused by the woman's permanently dark mood, with lyrics that string together references to classic blues and blues-rock songs by Elmore James, Jimi Hendrix, Cream, the Rolling Stones and more. It's a simple premise but is carried off with Roth's usual panache. The track starts softly, Roth crooning huskily over palm-muted minor chords. This builds to a catchy sixties pop-influenced bridge, with call-and-response harmonies worthy of the early Beatles. The dynamics lift again into the chorus, with Dave belting out impressive high notes, and Wolfgang and Eddie providing strong vocal backing. According to an interview with Wolfgang for *Ultimate Classic Rock*, Roth was keen to handle all the backing vocals himself, but:

There were a couple of songs we went back in and just said, 'Fuck it, we're gonna do this. It's part of it. He can't stop us.' It was Dad and I in the chorus, and that was really fun.

The stomping middle-eight is built on a riff that creeps up in chromatic increments, racking up the tension as Roth doubles his lead vocal line an octave lower. This leads into a blistering eight-bar solo and a full-pelt double chorus before fading out with a reprise of the moody intro riff. It's an excellent number that introduces a broader dynamic and emotional spectrum to the album and shows that however many archival gems they have in reserve, the band's ability to create new material of the same standard is beyond question.

'China Town' (Van Halen, Roth)

This fearsome rocker is a spectacular showcase for the band's collective musical prowess. The opening burst of wild two-handed tapping sounds like Eddie playing through an octave pedal, but is, in fact, father and son, shredding in unison with almost telepathic precision, Wolfgang playing a six-string bass. The track careers along on a wave of machine-gun double kick drums, with Eddie's guitar moving seamlessly between intense, thrashy chugging and bursts of chiming melody. Over this exhilarating backdrop, punctuated by sleazy wah-wah breakdowns, Roth paints a gritty noir scenario, setting the scene with a particularly grisly bit of wordplay ('Headless body in a topless bar') and developing from there. It's a grandstanding performance, with cinematic imagery and Chandlerian turn of phrase. Roth transitions easily from rattling out rapid-fire syllables in the verse to crooning melodiously through the bridge. Credit is also due to John Shanks here. He was very much known as a pop producer prior to this album but clearly knows how to capture the band's heavy side. There's no excessive varnish or gimmickry – just powerful playing, beautifully recorded. While the band's

129

1990s recordings suffer in retrospect from flawed attempts to keep up with contemporary sonic trends, by 2012, they had stopped trying to keep up with current fashions, and were content to simply be themselves. As a result, the likes of 'China Town', while not deviating far from the band's 1970s sonic template, sound far more vibrant and timeless than their ill-fated flirtations with grunge and nu-metal.

'Blood and Fire' (Van Halen, Roth)

This anthem of redemption and renewal began life as the instrumental, 'Ripley', which was part of Eddie's score to *The Wild Life* – the same score that provided the basis for 'Right Now'. The original title refers to the fact that the piece is played on the Ripley stereo guitar, previously heard on 'Top Jimmy'. By 2010, when recording commenced, the instrument had lain unused for years and had to be returned to its builder for repair. Its unique sound is evident on the arpeggiated introduction, with individual notes of each chord emerging at different points in the stereo spectrum. From this subtle beginning, the track quickly gathers momentum. There's a real sense of excitement palpable in Alex's sizzling wall of splashy ride cymbal and hyperactive fills, and Wolfgang's McCartney-esque octave swoops in the chorus. Roth's lyrics trace the band's tempestuous journey and odds-defying triumphant return. His performance is joyous and emotive – perhaps his best on the record, sounding genuinely moved to be back in his rightful place, as he quotes his own onstage catchphrase: 'Now look at all of the people here tonight'. The chiming, melodic middle eight leads to a brief breakdown section, with Roth wryly quipping, 'Told ya I was comin' back... say you missed me'. There follows an impassioned solo, with the cleaner tones of the Ripley guitar joined by a wall of overdriven rhythm guitars. A half-verse and a final all-guns-blazing chorus eventually simmer down into a wistful reprise of the gentle intro.

The original 'Ripley' track was little more than a couple of catchy riffs strung together. However, with the addition of Roth's words and top-notch ensemble performance, it is transformed into a latter-day classic – at once nostalgic, hopeful and triumphant.

'Bullethead'

This song, originally featured in the band's live sets back in 1977, was one of the first three that the reconfigured band reworked, the others being 'She's the Woman' and 'Let's Get Rockin'', later retitled 'Outta Space'. The success of these initial recordings gave the band the confidence to record a full album, something Eddie had been reluctant to do. As Wolfgang told *Ultimate Classic Rock*, 'When we did those three songs it was like, 'Oh shit, we can do this!'. 'Bullethead' is a high-energy up-tempo rocker – one of those early tunes, like 'Loss of Control' and 'Ain't Talkin' 'Bout Love' that responds to the nihilistic energy of the nascent LA punk scene. Musically, it's close to the

version heard on bootlegs from 1977 – two and a half minutes of headlong
chugging fury, its momentum only broken by a spikily-dissonant triplet
riff at the culmination of each chorus. Eddie's rhythm playing is powerful
and menacing, his leads brilliantly reckless, including a solo with a madly-
warbling fast chorus effect. The one major change from the song's original
incarnation is the lyrics. These now find Roth's narrator behind the wheel
and railing against the poor driving of a fellow road user – the 'bullethead' of
the title. In a broader sense, the song comments on the dangers of blinkered
stubbornness and offers a self-deprecating confession of Roth's own failings
in that area, wryly noting, 'Yes you are in danger, I drive just like you'. It's a
wonderfully snotty, snarky lyric, perfectly matching the attitudinal music, and
packed with puns, wordplay and Roth-isms that whizz by so fast they take
several listens to digest. It's a remarkable track – lean and fierce, recalling the
raw, edgy amphetamine buzz of Sunset Strip circa 1977 – not bad for three
near-pensioners and a kid just out of his teens!

'As Is' (Van Halen, Roth)

Perhaps the wildest track on the album, 'As Is' is a mostly-new composition,
although the main riff was heard briefly during Eddie's cameo on a 2009
episode of sitcom *Two and a Half Men*. This memorable appearance has
Eddie emerging from a bathroom brandishing his guitar, having apparently
just composed the riff on the toilet, announcing its title as 'Two Burritos and
a Root Beer Float'! The track starts with thunderous drums, soon joined by
a sludgy down-tuned riff. From this gargantuan intro, the 'Two Burritos' riff
emerges – a dazzling, bluesy blur of hammer-ons and pull-offs over a light-
footed kick, snare and hats beat, with the bass adding syncopated accents
at the end of each four-bar phrase. The sound fills out for the chorus, with
Alex's relentless double kicks pushing the track along and yelled gang vocals
adding to the rowdy atmosphere. The middle-eight is presaged by Dave's
spoken warning that 'This next part should really confuse things – everybody,
let's stay focused', and finds Wolfgang's bass descending to an almost sub-
sonic rumble – he played the track with his bottom E string tuned down by
at least a fifth, and the other three strings in standard tuning. After a hectic
instrumental which features some scorching minor-key tapping and a reprise
of the monolithic intro riff, there's a breakdown, with Eddie picking out
clean-toned blues licks and Dave growling out some classic Roth-isms: 'Love
'em all, I says, let Cupid sort 'em out!'. The track eventually fades out to the
chords of the middle-eight, with Roth singing a 'La la la' hook as Eddie layers
up guitars, using his vibrato bar to manipulate the pitch of warbling feedback.

The chaotic, careering music is matched by one of Dave's most madcap
lyrics, laced with puns and wisecracks but with a philosophical core. The lyric
draws inspiration from Dave's old Opel Kadett, the dilapidated vehicle he
bought and drove in 'as is' condition during his pre-fame days. After the band
became successful, he kept hold of the car, initially as a practical measure,

lest fame should be short-lived, and later as a totemistic gesture, eventually mounting it in his living room, with a deer coming through the windscreen! Reminiscing about the Opel sets Roth off on a scattershot riff on the nature of fame and fortune and the things that are important in creative and personal life: 'Love of the craft or love of the buck/ Every day down here's a rainy day, we don't save up'. 'As Is' isn't one of the album's obvious 'hits', but it's an entertaining and exciting record with a surprisingly thoughtful message behind Roth's gonzoid meanderings.

'Honeybabysweetiedoll' (Van Halen, Roth)

This unusual track is alleged by some to be based on an unreleased song from the *Women and Children First* sessions, although there's no evidence in the public domain to confirm this. It feels like a distant relation of 'Outta Love Again', with a similarly restless hard funk feel. However, 'Honeybabysweetiedoll' is both heavier and weirder than its *Van Halen II* cousin, featuring a vaguely middle eastern sounding riff based on the Phrygian mode, delivered with punishing Black Sabbath weight. Roth's lyrics are throwaway – a babbling stream of endearments and entreaties, including a few questionable metaphors ('I'm a face grenade with the sex pin pulled' anyone?). The real focus of the song is the ensemble playing of the Van Halen family. The track begins with a mess of radio static and electronic sounds, before the riff emerges, tapped out on Wolfgang's auto-wah-treated bass. Alex and Eddie soon join the fray, Eddie using a Whammy pedal to make some wild multi-octave pitch leaps in his lead fills. The band's playing is never less than thrilling, and there's plenty going on to hold the listener's interest, with all manner of unusual guitar and bass effects and even a brief cameo from Roth's pet dog. Nevertheless, as a song, it's considerably less fully realised than any of the album's other material, and is the least essential track on this strong record.

'The Trouble with Never' (Van Halen, Roth)

Van Halen have often employed elements of funk in their songs, but they've rarely leaned so hard into the genre as on this Hendrix-channelling wah-wah drenched strut. The flashy unison passages that make up the main riff and verse find guitar, bass and drums locked tight, using space and syncopation to create a danceable, hard-rocking groove. The chorus moves to a more four-square rhythm and major tonality, emphasised by some bright harmonies. A snarling wah guitar solo breaks down into a half-time section, with Roth growling huskily over minimal, menacing bass and drums. Eddie's guitar crashes back in, and the tempo picks back up for a raucous final chorus, concluding with some lithe funk riffing. Roth's words, as usual, give the appearance of shallow frivolity but conceal a philosophical enquiry. On one hand, the song is essentially a protracted pick-up line, with our narrator urging the object of his affection to never say never, asking 'When was the last time you did something for the first time?'. Really though, the lyrics are about human nature, and our tendency to limit our potential by closing ourselves off from new experiences: 'A simple question concerning time/ Suppose you wait forever, and then you change your mind?'. There are points at which it's a challenge for Dave to fit his wordy lyrics into the busy, restless music, but he manages it with a combination of *laissez faire* phrasing and sheer exuberance.

It's perhaps not the album's greatest song, but with tremendous playing, a lively and engaging vocal and catchy chorus, it's still a strong track.

'Outta Space' (Van Halen, Roth)

Of the album's revamped older songs, 'Outta Space' is perhaps musically closest to its original version. The instrumental track of the 1977 demo version, titled 'Let's Get Rockin'' is almost identical, save for a generally thinner sound, Michael Anthony's slightly more workmanlike bassline, and a different guitar solo, which is overdubbed over a rhythm track while 'Outta Space' only uses a single guitar. With its snarling riff and punky energy, the track sits comfortably alongside the band's rowdiest early numbers, starting at full blast and staying there. The verses find Roth belting powerfully at the top of his range, while the bridge breaks away from blues basics, with Dave singing a lower melodic line over adventurous chord changes. The momentum lets up briefly for the thudding stop-time chorus, with Eddie interjecting high lead shrieks in-between vocal phrases. The solo finds Eddie using his trusty MXR Phase 90 for the first time in a while, leaving the effect on through the brooding middle eight. There's an extra-musical tag at the end of the last bridge before a final curtailed chorus slams the track to a halt inside three breathless minutes.

Impressively, the 2012 incarnation of Van Halen sounds just as sprightly and aggressive here as the hungry young band of 1977 did on the original demo.

As with several other early demos, 'Let's Get Rockin'' had a great riff and plenty of good ideas but was let down by a relatively weak vocal melody and generic lyrics. 'Outta Space', gives rock cliches a wide berth, addressing the serious issues of over-population and the climate crisis, albeit in Dave's carefree, wisecracking style. The title has a double meaning; according to our narrator, humanity is out of space. The solution? Escape to outer space. There's a serious message buried in there, with the second verse noting, 'Eighty acres of non-stop shopping has somewhat changed the place', and the narrator confessing, 'I am guilty, I do use it'. However, Roth isn't one to get bogged down in self-recrimination or catastrophism and manages to make escaping the ruined earth sound fun and exciting.

A great track, then, and one that shows that, rather than merely living off their legacy by revisiting old demos, the band are elevating those early songs and adding contemporary relevance to boot.

'Stay Frosty' (Van Halen, Roth)

The band revisits the country-blues-turned-boogie-blowout stylings of 'Ice Cream Man' for this track, which is a veritable Roth *tour de force*. Like the aforementioned classic, 'Stay Frosty' begins intimately, with Roth accompanying himself on acoustic guitar, with some impressively nimble walking bass runs and melodic touches. After two verses and choruses, the rest of the band bursts in with heavy-duty backing, Alex breaking out his trademark double-kick shuffle for the first time in years. Unlike 'Ice Cream Man', Dave keeps his acoustic accompaniment going, his mellow strumming contrasting nicely with Eddie's raw electric power. There are two fine guitar solos, the first a blast of hot blues preceding the final chorus, and the second an outro piece, leading into a mean-sounding down-tuned boogie riff before an epic crash ending. According to Eddie in *Eruption,* 'Wolfgang came up with the arrangement for 'Stay Frosty'. When Dave wrote it, it was just an acoustic thing like it is on the intro. Wolf turned it into what it is'. It's a measure of the band's improved ability to collaborate and of how far Dave and Eddie had reined in their respective egos that the young bassist was able to participate as a creative equal. In fact, Wolf's influence was vital throughout the sessions, not just as a musician but as a creative catalyst and moderating influence, his presence perhaps reminding the rest of the band that they were, in fact, grown-ups!

The lyrics are a tongue-in-cheek philosophical treatise. Dave takes an epic voyage of self-discovery, consulting leaders of the world's major religions for spiritual guidance and receiving the same advice from each: 'stay frosty'. As you'd expect, the journey is narrated with customary wise-ass wit but also conveys something of Roth's personal beliefs; namely that there are no certainties in life, so you need to figure out your own path, remaining cautiously sceptical of easy answers, or as his Rabbi says, 'God guides us on our journey, but careful with those feet!'. It's terrific fun, tapping into the boisterous spirit and humour of the band's early work and adding a touch of philosophy, as befits a band who have lived hard and learned a few things about life along the way.

'Big River' (Van Halen, Roth)

Originally heard on the Gene Simmons demo as 'Big Trouble', this is another track that remains musically close to its 1970s counterpart. The distinctive baroque-sounding picked intro, bold main riff and contrasting instrumental chord sequence were all in place back in 1976. However, the original lyrics, depicting a young couple caught *in flagrante delicto* by the girl's father, weren't terrific, to begin with, and would have been positively inappropriate for a singer rapidly approaching 60. Dave's new words are a minimal, poetic and almost abstract hymn to the Charles River, the same Massachusetts waterway that inspired The Standells' 1966 garage-punk classic, 'Dirty Water'. The band take the song at a statelier pace than the original demo, with hi-hat

16ths driving the track along while a thumping whole-note bass pedal point maintains an even keel. The track's huge sound and steady-but-unstoppable motion mirror the titular river, with things only getting a little choppy in the instrumental. Here, the track moves to a darker minor key, with funky syncopation in the rhythm section. Eddie's solo is fierce, building to a burst of incendiary tapping before smoothly diverting back to the main riff for a last chorus and long fade-out. There is less complexity to 'Big River' than some of the album's other songs, but it's a mightily impressive-sounding record with an intriguing, Zen-like lyric, taking the essence of the 1976 demo and turning it into something much more powerful.

'Beats Workin'' (Van Halen, Roth)

The last track on Van Halen's final studio album again dates back to the 1976 demo. Its original incarnation was titled 'Put Out the Lights', and its bump n' grind groove was married to cringeworthy lyrics concerning 'Fast Eddie' and his 'Little lady'. 'Beats Workin'' retains the demo's riff and basic structure but adds a new monolithic instrumental introduction, giving the song's opening a Black Sabbath-like sense of drama. As with the other reworked demos, it's Dave who has the most to do. Gone are the tales of Fast Eddie's amorous exploits, replaced by a meditation on the tenuous nature of rock stardom, and the combination of talent and dumb luck on which it hinges. In typical Roth style, the punning title carries two meanings. For much of the song, it's referring to a drumbeat, having the desired effect of making the listener want to dance: 'Beat's workin'/ Startin' up all in my feet'. At the same time, it's also a statement that playing in a rock band is preferable to joining the regular workforce. Along with the new lyric, Dave has come up with a fresh melody and a catchier chorus hook. He delivers a belting, charismatic performance that takes him to the very top of his range and overdubs some terrific harmonies, which don't quite compensate for the absence of Mike's voice but come pretty close.

After the epic intro, the song alternates between a forceful mid-tempo drive and a half-time hip-swinging groove. Of all the reworked songs, this is the one that wears its 1970s origins most clearly on its sleeve. There's an old-school sleazy Sunset Strip vibe that is entirely fitting, bringing the band's sound full circle on their final track. The instrumental begins with Eddie playing a composed melodic line, which leads into a great bass breakdown, showcasing Wolfgang's nimble fretwork and huge, growling tone. Eddie plays a wah-wah-laced solo over this new riff, which builds to a crescendo, followed by a final chorus. Eddie keeps soloing, ending the album with a last feedback divebomb. It's not the most substantial song on the album, but it makes for a pleasing finale, capturing the combination of unbelievable musicianship and raunchy frivolity that made the band so irresistible in the first place.

Tokyo Dome In Concert (2015)

Personnel:
David Lee Roth: lead vocals, acoustic guitar on 'Ice Cream Man'
Edward Van Halen: guitar, backing vocals
Wolfgang Van Halen: bass, backing vocals
Alex Van Halen: drums
Additional personnel:
Alan Fitzgerald – Keyboards? (credited as Keyboard Technician)
Recorded at Tokyo Dome, Tokyo, Japan, 21 June 2013
Produced by Van Halen
Mixed by Bob Clearmountain
Record label: Warner Brothers
Release date: 26 January 1993
Highest chart position: US: 20, UK: 74
Running time: 119:52
Current edition: Rhino Records CD reissue
Tracklisting: 'Unchained', 'Runnin' with the Devil', 'She's the Woman', 'I'm the One', 'Tattoo', 'Everybody Wants Some!!', 'Somebody Get Me a Doctor', 'China Town', 'Hear About it Later', '(Oh) Pretty Woman', 'Me & You (Drum Solo)', 'You Really Got Me', 'Dance the Night Away', I'll Wait', 'And the Cradle Will Rock', 'Hot For Teacher', 'Women in Love', 'Romeo Delight', 'Mean Street', 'Beautiful Girls', Ice Cream Man', 'Panama', 'Eruption', 'Ain't Talkin' 'Bout Love', 'Jump'

When the *A Different Kind of Truth* tour concluded, the band considered a few options for their next release. Although the long-term goal was to make a new studio record, that wasn't going to happen any time soon, so other possibilities were contemplated for a stop-gap release. Initially, the band considered officially releasing the 1977 Warner Brothers demo, but that idea was dismissed when it emerged that the original tapes had been lost. The next thought was to release a live recording from the band's early years. A number of early shows had been recorded for radio broadcasts, but while the sound quality of these widely bootlegged recordings is far from unlistenable, it didn't meet Eddie's exacting standards, and his attempts to enhance the sound technologically robbed the recordings of their essential atmosphere. Instead, they decided on a live album from the most recent tour. The band had recorded every show from the 2007 reunion tour onwards, so there were plenty to choose from. In a gesture that showed how much the dynamic within the band had improved, Eddie gave Dave freedom to choose which performances would be featured. In *Eruption,* he explains his decision thus:

Performing live is a lot harder on a singer. Wolfgang and I sing backup vocals on the choruses, so we know how much the vocals can vary from one night to the next. When your voice is your instrument, it can be affected by a lot of different things. If you sleep with the air conditioner on or the bus ride is too long, you can wake up the next day with a fucked-up voice. That's the main reason we decided to let Dave pick.

The show Roth chose was the 21 June performance from the Tokyo Dome, 'in front of 44,000 of our closest friends', as the sleeve notes say. Roth is a sometime Tokyo resident, so the show had a special significance for him. He certainly sounds delighted to be there, and even conducts some of his stage banter in Japanese. While the band's first live album was extensively reworked in the studio, to the point where it was barely 'live' at all, they took the opposite approach with *Tokyo Dome In Concert*. Rather than re-recording or fixing anything, Eddie simply turned the recordings over to veteran engineer, Bob Clearmountain for mixing, ensuring an authentic 'warts and all' representation of the live experience. The setlist is a solid selection of hits and favourites from 1978-84, plus three songs from *A Different Kind of Truth* and solo spots for Eddie and Alex. The only title that has not appeared on a previous Van Halen album is 'Me & You', retitled 'Drum Struck' for digital releases. Rather than an actual song, this is Alex's drum solo, played over a pre-recorded Latin American-influenced backing. It's entertaining enough, if inessential, and benefits from its relatively concise length. Otherwise, it's a great, high-energy set, capturing superb playing from the band, with Wolf sounding particularly impressive as he puts his own spin on the old songs while capably handling Anthony's backing vocal parts (Roth evens breaks off from his lead vocal to compliment him in the middle of a rampant 'I'm the One')! Eddie plays guitar throughout, and nobody is credited with keyboards, yet keyboard parts are present where required. These may be pre-recorded, but as ex-Night Ranger keyboardist Alan Fitzgerald is credited as 'Keyboard technician', it seems safe to assume that he is playing the parts offstage, as he did for *Live: Right Here, Right Now*.

Throughout, Roth is as unpredictable as ever, reinterpreting songs on the fly and dropping in often hilarious, occasionally baffling spoken non-sequiturs. Several critics were quick to pounce on Roth's vocal performance, with embittered former singer, Sammy Hagar at the forefront, commenting to the *Las Vegas Review Journal*: 'They've got some pretty rough vocals... Every time they do something, I'm like, 'Oh my god, can these guys do anything worse to their reputation and to the level of the music of the band?''. Really, Hagar and the other naysayers are missing the point. A Roth-era Van Halen show was never about studio-quality performances. Recordings from the classic era reveal that Dave hardly ever sang a song live as it was on record, often skipping lines to perform leaps or dance moves, scatting his way through sections, or occasionally stopping singing altogether with a bellow of 'I forgot the fuckin' words!'. Roth could have gone back to the studio and re-sung everything, but anyone who had ever heard him perform with the band would have seen through the artifice. Far better to have a well-recorded and mixed representation of exactly what the audience at the show heard, in all its spontaneous ragged glory.

Continuing the previous album's 'awe-inspiring images of vintage transport' theme, the cover of the two-CD/ four-LP set featured a 1935 poster image of the ocean liner SS Normandie, painted by French commercial artist Cassandre. The album reached number 20 on the *Billboard* chart – not bad for an intended stop-gap release before an eventual new studio album. Eddie continued to cling to this plan as his health worsened and even made some moves towards organising a tour which would finally bury long-standing resentments, uniting all members of Van Halen, past and present, in a single extravaganza. Sadly, this would never come to fruition. Eddie and family kept his health issues private, but troubling rumours inevitably surfaced, and on the sixth of October 2020, Wolfgang announced that his father had passed away from cancer. There was no question of the band continuing without their visionary musical leader, so *Tokyo Dome In Concert* remains their final recorded statement – a flawed, human, exciting and hugely entertaining summary of an astonishing career.

Other Van Halen releases

In addition to the albums detailed here, there have been a few Van Halen releases for visual media containing unique recordings. The first of these was *Live Without a Net* (1986), a 90-minute document of the band's performance at the Veteran's Memorial Coliseum, New Haven, Connecticut from 27 August of that year. This home video release documents a typical *5150* tour set – low on Roth-era songs, high on new-album content, and featuring Van Halen-ised versions of a couple of Hagar hits. There's also a raucous bash through Led Zeppelin's 'Rock n' Roll' for an encore. It's not the greatest setlist, but the performance is fantastic, and the film captures the giddy excitement of this new chapter in the band's history. It's also interesting to see the band handling the keyboard-based songs prior to hiring an offstage session player, with Sammy taking over guitar duties as Eddie moves to the synth. While the film has been reissued on DVD, it seems odd that an accompanying album has never been issued, as many fans would love to have an audio document of this great show.

There was also a DVD release of *Live: Right Here, Right Now*, including versions of 'The Dream is Over' and 'Eagles Fly' which were absent from the album, although 'Eagles Fly' did make it onto the bonus disc of the German and Japanese releases. Unfortunately, after the amount of post-production work that was done on the audio, there was little chance of the video footage syncing up. As a result, the film jumps back and forth between footage from two different concerts, making it feel more like a massively-extended promo video than a representation of an actual concert experience.

Moving ahead a few years, the deluxe edition of *A Different Kind of Truth* came with a DVD entitled *The Downtown Sessions*, featuring acoustic versions of 'Panama', 'You and Your Blues' and 'Beautiful Girls', filmed in black and white. There's a fun, loose knockabout feel to these versions, with Alex providing somewhat chaotic accompaniment on bongos and congas, and Dave on especially silly form. He gives a lengthy spoken introduction to 'You and Your Blues', and is clearly having a fine time, his dog occasionally wandering into shot in-between takes as the band sit in a semi-circle, chuckling or groaning at quips. Though far from essential, it's enjoyable seeing and hearing the band in a relaxed, intimate setting, so far removed from the arena shows that they would generally play.

With Eddie's tragic death, we can be sure Van Halen won't be recording any new music, but there's still a possibility of archive releases. Although Eddie nixed the idea of releasing the Warners demo due to the loss of the original tapes, it's hard to believe a good engineer couldn't make a release-worthy master from a secondary source. Although the demo has been widely available for years, originally on bootlegs and now on the internet, any fan would relish an official release, properly mastered and well-packaged. Hopefully, this is something Warner Brothers and the Van Halen estate will consider in the future. But why stop there? Given the decades' worth of fascinating demos which have never been officially released, why not a series of albums or a box set? Many would be interested in proper releases of the Gene Simmons demo, the 1974 recordings with Mark Stone (their historical value offsetting poor sound quality), and even the aborted second Gary Cherone album. The estates of Prince and Frank Zappa, among others have provided perfect examples of how to create beautifully-curated posthumous archive releases, and we can only hope that, in time, the Van Halen estate may follow suit.

On Track series

Allman Brothers Band – Andrew Wild 978-1-78952-252-5
Tori Amos – Lisa Torem 978-1-78952-142-9
Asia – Peter Braidis 978-1-78952-099-6
Badfinger – Robert Day-Webb 978-1-878952-176-4
Barclay James Harvest – Keith and Monica Domone 978-1-78952-067-5
The Beatles – Andrew Wild 978-1-78952-009-5
The Beatles Solo 1969-1980 – Andrew Wild 978-1-78952-030-9
Blue Oyster Cult – Jacob Holm-Lupo 978-1-78952-007-1
Blur – Matt Bishop 978-178952-164-1
Marc Bolan and T.Rex – Peter Gallagher 978-1-78952-124-5
Kate Bush – Bill Thomas 978-1-78952-097-2
Camel – Hamish Kuzminski 978-1-78952-040-8
Captain Beefheart – Opher Goodwin 978-1-78952-235-8
Caravan – Andy Boot 978-1-78952-127-6
Cardiacs – Eric Benac 978-1-78952-131-3
Nick Cave and The Bad Seeds – Dominic Sanderson 978-1-78952-240-2
Eric Clapton Solo – Andrew Wild 978-1-78952-141-2
The Clash – Nick Assirati 978-1-78952-077-4
Crosby, Stills and Nash – Andrew Wild 978-1-78952-039-2
Creedence Clearwater Revival – Tony Thompson 978-178952-237-2
The Damned – Morgan Brown 978-1-78952-136-8
Deep Purple and Rainbow 1968-79 – Steve Pilkington 978-1-78952-002-6
Dire Straits – Andrew Wild 978-1-78952-044-6
The Doors – Tony Thompson 978-1-78952-137-5
Dream Theater – Jordan Blum 978-1-78952-050-7
Eagles – John Van der Kiste 978-1-78952-260-0
Electric Light Orchestra – Barry Delve 978-1-78952-152-8
Elvis Costello and The Attractions – Georg Purvis 978-1-78952-129-0
Emerson Lake and Palmer – Mike Goode 978-1-78952-000-2
Fairport Convention – Kevan Furbank 978-1-78952-051-4
Peter Gabriel – Graeme Scarfe 978-1-78952-138-2
Genesis – Stuart MacFarlane 978-1-78952-005-7
Gentle Giant – Gary Steel 978-1-78952-058-3
Gong – Kevan Furbank 978-1-78952-082-8
Hall and Oates – Ian Abrahams 978-1-78952-167-2
Hawkwind – Duncan Harris 978-1-78952-052-1
Peter Hammill – Richard Rees Jones 978-1-78952-163-4
Roy Harper – Opher Goodwin 978-1-78952-130-6
Jimi Hendrix – Emma Stott 978-1-78952-175-7
The Hollies – Andrew Darlington 978-1-78952-159-7
The Human League and The Sheffield Scene – Andrew Darlington 978-1-78952-186-3
Iron Maiden – Steve Pilkington 978-1-78952-061-3
Jefferson Airplane – Richard Butterworth 978-1-78952-143-6
Jethro Tull – Jordan Blum 978-1-78952-016-3
Elton John in the 1970s – Peter Kearns 978-1-78952-034-7
The Incredible String Band – Tim Moon 978-1-78952-107-8
Iron Maiden – Steve Pilkington 978-1-78952-061-3
Joe Jackson – Richard James 978-1-78952-189-4
Billy Joel – Lisa Torem 978-1-78952-183-2
Judas Priest – John Tucker 978-1-78952-018-7
Kansas – Kevin Cummings 978-1-78952-057-6
The Kinks – Martin Hutchinson 978-1-78952-172-6
Korn – Matt Karpe 978-1-78952-153-5
Led Zeppelin – Steve Pilkington 978-1-78952-151-1

Also available from Sonicbond

Level 42 – Matt Philips 978-1-78952-102-3
Little Feat – Georg Purvis - 978-1-78952-168-9
Aimee Mann – Jez Rowden 978-1-78952-036-1
Joni Mitchell – Peter Kearns 978-1-78952-081-1
The Moody Blues – Geoffrey Feakes 978-1-78952-042-2
Motorhead – Duncan Harris 978-1-78952-173-3
Nektar – Scott Meze – 978-1-78952-257-0
New Order – Dennis Remmer – 979-1-78952-249-5
Laura Nyro – Philip Ward 978-1-78952-182-5
Mike Oldfield – Ryan Yard 978-1-78952-060-6
Opeth – Jordan Blum 978-1-78-952-166-5
Pearl Jam – Ben L. Connor 978-1-78952-188-7
Tom Petty – Richard James 978-1-78952-128-3
Pink Floyd – 978-1-78952-242-6 Richard Butterworth
Porcupine Tree – Nick Holmes 978-1-78952-144-3
Queen – Andrew Wild 978-1-78952-003-3
Radiohead – William Allen 978-1-78952-149-8
Rancid – Paul Matts 989-1-78952-187-0
Renaissance – David Detmer 978-1-78952-062-0
The Rolling Stones 1963-80 – Steve Pilkington 978-1-78952-017-0
The Smiths and Morrissey – Tommy Gunnarsson 978-1-78952-140-5
Spirit – Rev. Keith A. Gordon – 978-1-78952- 248-8
Stackridge – Alan Draper 978-1-78952-232-7
Status Quo the Frantic Four Years – Richard James 978-1-78952-160-3
Steely Dan – Jez Rowden 978-1-78952-043-9
Steve Hackett – Geoffrey Feakes 978-1-78952-098-9
Tears For Fears – Paul Clark - 978-178952-238-9
Thin Lizzy – Graeme Stroud 978-1-78952-064-4
Tool – Matt Karpe 978-1-78952-234-1
Toto – Jacob Holm-Lupo 978-1-78952-019-4
U2 – Eoghan Lyng 978-1-78952-078-1
UFO – Richard James 978-1-78952-073-6
Van Der Graaf Generator – Dan Coffey 978-1-78952-031-6
Van Halen – Morgan Brown – 9781-78952-256-3
The Who – Geoffrey Feakes 978-1-78952-076-7
Roy Wood and the Move – James R Turner 978-1-78952-008-8
Yes – Stephen Lambe 978-1-78952-001-9
Frank Zappa 1966 to 1979 – Eric Benac 978-1-78952-033-0
Warren Zevon – Peter Gallagher 978-1-78952-170-2
10CC – Peter Kearns 978-1-78952-054-5

Decades Series
The Bee Gees in the 1960s – Andrew Mon Hughes et al 978-1-78952-148-1
The Bee Gees in the 1970s – Andrew Mon Hughes et al 978-1-78952-179-5
Black Sabbath in the 1970s – Chris Sutton 978-1-78952-171-9
Britpop – Peter Richard Adams and Matt Pooler 978-1-78952-169-6
Phil Collins in the 1980s – Andrew Wild 978-1-78952-185-6
Alice Cooper in the 1970s – Chris Sutton 978-1-78952-104-7
Curved Air in the 1970s – Laura Shenton 978-1-78952-069-9
Donovan in the 1960s – Jeff Fitzgerald 978-1-78952-233-4
Bob Dylan in the 1980s – Don Klees 978-1-78952-157-3
Brian Eno in the 1970s – Gary Parsons 978-1-78952-239-6
Faith No More in the 1990s – Matt Karpe 978-1-78952-250-1
Fleetwood Mac in the 1970s – Andrew Wild 978-1-78952-105-4
Fleetwood Mac in the 1980s – Don Klees 978-178952-254-9

Focus in the 1970s – Stephen Lambe 978-1-78952-079-8
Free and Bad Company in the 1970s – John Van der Kiste 978-1-78952-178-8
Genesis in the 1970s – Bill Thomas 978178952-146-7
George Harrison in the 1970s – Eoghan Lyng 978-1-78952-174-0
Kiss in the 1970s – Peter Gallagher 978-1-78952-246-4
Manfred Mann's Earth Band in the 1970s – John Van der Kiste 978178952-243-3
Marillion in the 1980s – Nathaniel Webb 978-1-78952-065-1
Van Morrison in the 1970s – Peter Childs - 978-1-78952-241-9
Mott the Hoople and Ian Hunter in the 1970s – John Van der Kiste 978-1-78-952-162-7
Pink Floyd In The 1970s – Georg Purvis 978-1-78952-072-9
Suzi Quatro in the 1970s – Darren Johnson 978-1-78952-236-5
Roxy Music in the 1970s – Dave Thompson 978-1-78952-180-1
Status Quo in the 1980s – Greg Harper 978-1-78952-244-0
Tangerine Dream in the 1970s – Stephen Palmer 978-1-78952-161-0
The Sweet in the 1970s – Darren Johnson 978-1-78952-139-9
Uriah Heep in the 1970s – Steve Pilkington 978-1-78952-103-0
Van der Graaf Generator in the 1970s – Steve Pilkington 978-1-78952-245-7
Yes in the 1980s – Stephen Lambe with David Watkinson 978-1-78952-125-2

On Screen series
Carry On... – Stephen Lambe 978-1-78952-004-0
David Cronenberg – Patrick Chapman 978-1-78952-071-2
Doctor Who: The David Tennant Years – Jamie Hailstone 978-1-78952-066-8
James Bond – Andrew Wild 978-1-78952-010-1
Monty Python – Steve Pilkington 978-1-78952-047-7
Seinfeld Seasons 1 to 5 – Stephen Lambe 978-1-78952-012-5

Other Books
1967: A Year In Psychedelic Rock 978-1-78952-155-9
1970: A Year In Rock – John Van der Kiste 978-1-78952-147-4
1973: The Golden Year of Progressive Rock 978-1-78952-165-8
Babysitting A Band On The Rocks – G.D. Praetorius 978-1-78952-106-1
Eric Clapton Sessions – Andrew Wild 978-1-78952-177-1
Derek Taylor: For Your Radioactive Children – Andrew Darlington 978-1-78952-038-5
The Golden Road: The Recording History of The Grateful Dead – John Kilbride 978-1-78952-156-6
Iggy and The Stooges On Stage 1967-1974 – Per Nilsen 978-1-78952-101-6
Jon Anderson and the Warriors – the road to Yes – David Watkinson 978-1-78952-059-0
Misty: The Music of Johnny Mathis – Jakob Baekgaard 978-1-78952-247-1
Nu Metal: A Definitive Guide – Matt Karpe 978-1-78952-063-7
Tommy Bolin: In and Out of Deep Purple – Laura Shenton 978-1-78952-070-5
Maximum Darkness – Deke Leonard 978-1-78952-048-4
The Twang Dynasty – Deke Leonard 978-1-78952-049-1

and many more to come!

Would you like to write for Sonicbond Publishing?

At Sonicbond Publishing we are always on the look-out for authors,
particularly for our two main series:

On Track. Mixing fact with in depth analysis, the On Track series
examines the work of a particular musical artist or group. All genres
are considered from easy listening and jazz to 60s soul to 90s pop,
via rock and metal.

On Screen. This series looks at the world of film and television. Sub-
jects considered include directors, actors and writers, as well as entire
television and film series. As with the On Track series, we balance
fact with analysis.

While professional writing experience would, of course, be an advan-
tage the most important qualification is to have real enthusiasm and
knowledge of your subject. First-time authors are welcomed, but the
ability to write well in English is essential.

Sonicbond Publishing has distribution throughout Europe and North
America, and all books are also published in E-book form. Authors
will be paid a royalty based on sales of their book.

Further details are available from www.sonicbondpublishing.co.uk.
To contact us, complete the contact form there or
email info@sonicbondpublishing.co.uk